Open to Outcome

A Practical Guide for Facilitating & Teaching Experiential Reflection

BY
MICAH JACOBSON & MARI RUDDY

Published by:

Wood 'N' Barnes Publishing & Distribution
2717 NW 50th, Oklahoma City, OK 73112
(405) 942-6812

Cover Design by Blue Design
Photography by Blue Design
Copyediting, Interior Design & Layout by Ramona Cunningham

Printed in the United States of America
Oklahoma City, Oklahoma
ISBN # 1-885473-59-1

Acknowledgments • • • • • • • • • • • • • • • • •

This book could not have been written without the dedication, thought, and brilliance of our colleague and friend, Mary Beth Campbell. Mary Beth served with us at every stage of the creation of this book, from development of the concept through initial draft editing. We are deeply indebted. Carolyn Hill also helped tremendously with these ideas and has presented them with incredible effectiveness for several years.

Many of the concepts for this book were created through our mutual contact with and work for the Link Crew and WEB programs. Phil Boyte created both programs and has served as a mentor and adviser to us for years. We are thankful for the opportunities, guidance, and friendship he always provided.

We received tremendous support from the thousands of Link Crew and WEB teachers who have been through our workshops. They are the champions working to make schools better places for kids. We especially thank Jeff Park, Jolene Kemos, Kate Thomason, Joanie Funderburk, and Chellie McCourt for reading early drafts and providing feedback and encouragement.

A book is just a dream until it is written and published. And this book might well have stayed a dream if not for Mony Cunningham and Dave Wood of Wood 'N' Barnes Publishing. We are thankful for their patience, persistence, and belief in our ability to write our ideas.

Finally, Jessica Jacobson, Jeanie Jacobson, Moe Jacobson, Marty, Maureen, Ginner and Tom Ruddy, Chris Klebl, Paul Williams, and Kylea Taylor have all our love. We would not be who we are without their love and support.

Endorsements for *Open to Outcome*:

"The 5 Questions just work! I couldn't believe how my group actually got the point when I just asked the questions!"

—Andy, Senior, Vintage High School

"Mari and Micah know adolescence. I have watched them work, and their skill and intuition is obvious. They have not only crafted a successful facilitation technique, they have applied it to an age group that is so often isolated. *Open to Outcome* provides teachers, coaches, and group leaders the insights and the questions to transform learning for youth. It demands the full participation and integrity of the participant learners, a vital element if the input is to be lasting and transformative."

—Dr. Terry Kneisler, Superintendent, Reynolds School District, Fairview, OR

"Ruddy and Jacobsen live the principles at the heart of experiential learning and articulate them in a way that can be applied with versatility in any group context. *Open to Outcome* is an easily understood and accessed touchstone to help facilitators stay on point, stay in close relationship with their group, and remain open to learning themselves. I will be recommending this book."

—Kylea Taylor, M.S., M.F.T., author of *The Ethics of Caring*

"The *Open to Outcome* in-service session was energizing, humorous, and thought-provoking. Teachers appreciated the researched-based approach to engaging students in dialogue instead of allowing them to be passive observers. The 5 Questions model is a simple, easy-to-use process for every classroom situation." —Jim Bennet, Principal, Lemoore High School, CA

"I use The 5 Questions model almost every day in my classroom. Amazingly, I now have begun to observe students using it on themselves! This process has truly transformed my teaching."

—Erin Noyes, Health Teacher, Olympia High School, WA

"The 5 Questions are important to examine after any situation because life is learning as you go along. It is important to stop and ask yourself what you learned from a particular experience. You learn by applying past lessons/experiences to current and future situations."

—Eileen Cronin, Graduate, St. Mary's College

Contents

Introduction

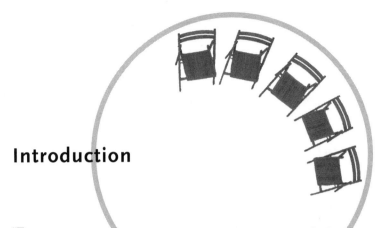

"THERE IS NOTHING SO EASY TO LEARN AS EXPERIENCE AND NOTHING SO HARD TO APPLY." —Josh Billings

"Open to Outcome" invites both new and experienced facilitators and teachers to explore and build effective methods for facilitating reflective debriefing with groups. In particular, we want to introduce the model we call "The 5 Questions."

As trainers for the nationally recognized Link Crew freshman orientation and transition program, and in a variety of other settings, we have many opportunities to work with students and educators using experiential activities and The 5 Questions. In every instance the goal is to facilitate and explore the incredible potential of teaching and learning experientially. Like many of you, we have taken our share of bumps and bruises along the way. Fortunately, those experiences were balanced with incredible successes and powerful learning moments that continue to influence and shape our lives.

What have we learned, as facilitators, about the process of learning? First, we found that experiential learning engages students and teachers in a way that is genuine and affects them where they live. When people get up and move, whether in games, icebreakers, team-building exercises, simulations, initiatives, internships, or just in living life, opportunities exist to learn profound lessons. A skilled facilitator, asking the right questions and guiding reflective conversation before, during, and after an experience, can help open a gateway to powerful new thinking and learning.

Second, the process of questioning needed to achieve this powerful learning is difficult to execute. We tried a variety of learning cycle approaches and found them either too conceptual for immediate application or too simple to create profound learning in the hands of moderately skilled facilitators.

This led us to create our own question model based on our beliefs about learning and learning cycles. The 5 Questions model is straightforward enough to teach to high school students for immediate application, yet still comprehensive enough to allow facilitation of complex activities. As we developed this model, a number of other related concepts emerged that influenced how we work with groups and how we wrote this book.

The Basic Idea
The 5 Questions model and related methods explored in "Open to Outcome" will equip facilitators to guide participants toward internal reflection. Participants will discover the learning that is true for them, not a predetermined outcome decided for them by the facilitator.

The challenge of being open to outcome is two-fold. The **first** challenge is for the facilitator to resist the temptation of imposing a particular learning and/or having a specific desired outcome for an activity. The **second** challenge in this approach is for the facilitator to remain open to the direction of the group or individual's learning without losing focus of the experience and coming to no learning at all.

The more deeply the facilitator understands The 5 Questions model, the more skill the facilitator will have to bring the group back to the experience and guide them to reflect on what it means for them and what they can take from it.

How is this Approach Different?
Perhaps the greatest distinction comes from the model's understanding and use of the verbs "to teach" and "to coach." These are complex verbs in the sense that each of them actually encompasses many other verbs within their definitions and they are often used interchangeably. For us, these two verbs are very distinct.

What is it to teach someone? For us the fundamental definition of "teaching" is communicating new information. Talking, telling, lecturing, and demonstrating are some of the actions used in achieving this goal.

Alternatively, what is it to coach someone? "Coaching," by our definition, is the process of reflecting on and expanding an idea or skill that has been previously learned.

In other words, once you have been taught a piece of information or a skill, you can then be coached to develop your thoughts about it or improve your ability to use it. The 5 Questions model supports the teaching/coaching process by providing a flexible structure for dialogue that facilitators working with groups or individuals can use to examine and reflect on an experience. The ultimate goal is that each individual or group, through reflection and coaching, will realize a profound and unique learning that will modify their future behavior.

Why does this distinction between coaching and teaching matter in facilitation? Because facilitators, during the debrief of an experience, should be doing more coaching and less teaching. They should be carefully observing participant behavior, guiding reflective conversation, and encouraging the application of what is learned. Beginning facilitators may slip unknowingly into teaching mode, telling the participants what they should have learned (e.g., "This exercise was about teamwork"). The goal should be to help participants uncover the learning that is paramount for them.

Exploring The 5 Questions Model
In this book we will explain why we crafted each question, why we ask them in the order we ask them, and the mental mind-sets we use when we ask them.

In Chapter 1, we talk about learning. This chapter summarizes what we have discovered about how learning occurs. Using theoretical models by Kolb and Piaget to modern brain research, we attempt to highlight the critical pieces of how people actually learn.

In Chapter 2, we discuss the mental mind-sets we have discovered that assist us in being the best facilitators possible. This chapter is about setting up powerful debriefings in such a way that problems and challenges are prevented before they occur.

In Chapter 3, we give you The 5 Questions model: Knowing where the questions come from and how they are intended to create powerful reflection and learning. Each question is analyzed to help you understand why it was developed and what purpose it serves in moving the conversation forward.

In Chapter 4, we outline strategies to keep the conversation moving. Of course, no amount of preventative work can anticipate every possibility. Chapter 4 is a tool kit for dealing with difficult issues and keeping a group on track.

In Chapter 5, we present The 5 Questions model workshop we have given to educators, facilitators, and students over the years for you to use with your own groups.

One final note: No process is foolproof. Although we continue to use and find success with our style and method of facilitating, please know we are not offering it as a panacea. We see The 5 Questions model and many of the other techniques in this book as tools rather than solutions. Tools work extremely effectively when used in the right way, in the right context, on the right problem. Trying to use a hammer when a saw is required will be frustrating for you and the hammer. We encourage you to pay attention to what works for you and what doesn't. Please let us know how it goes. We are eager to learn from you and will do what we can to help you become successful!

Chapter One | What is Learning?

"LEARN YOUR THEORIES AS WELL AS YOU CAN, BUT PUT
THEM ASIDE WHEN YOU TOUCH THE MIRACLE OF THE
LIVING SOUL." —Carl Jung

The Quick-Start Guide to Human Understanding and Learning

The 5 Questions model is founded in both brain-based learning strategies and theories about facilitating experiences based on stages. Understanding the stages of learning will raise the potential for creating a more powerful facilitation of The 5 Questions.

A brief survey of everyone you know will most likely reveal that among the top five moments of learning in their lives, at least four did not take place in the classroom. The learning that really sticks, that comes to guide us in times of crisis, is learned through our own experiences. Micah can still vividly recall learning the satisfaction of sharing by getting the "best passer" award as a 6-year-old in AYSO soccer. Mari remembers her family moving across the country when she was in third grade. She learned the pain of saying good-bye for the first time when she left her childhood best friend, and she also learned the possibilities for new friends. You may recall memories of an experience that taught you a lesson you have never forgotten.

Learning is tricky. We learn a lot of things throughout our lives that we rarely use and even more that we have completely forgotten. Then there are those learning moments that stand out as pivotal – when you learn a lesson that forever remains with you. Think about yourself for a moment. Who taught you about kindness? What did that experience look like? How did you learn the value of money?

Micah remembers learning the value of money for the first time. When he was 10, his mother gave him a $20 bill and sent him to the grocery store on his bike. Micah lost it on the way. He knew it was a big deal, but was not prepared for the search his mother made him undertake. Together they searched each grain of sand between their house and the grocery store. They never did find the money. But Micah never forgot that experience or how much his mother valued the money. He learned that money was not something to be taken lightly. A completely different learning would have occurred if Micah's mother had simply shrugged it off and taken him back to the grocery store. Each experience in our lives leaves an imprint that helps us shape the way we view, exist in, and interact with the world.

The term "experiential learning" can be applied to everything from on-the-job training to structured simulations in a workshop environment. It could be argued that everything that happens in our lives is ultimately an experience. However, we believe it is important to differentiate experiential learning from abstracted text learning or lecture-based learning. We are specifically writing for facilitators and teachers who use simulations, initiatives, games, and activities in the classroom and want to process those experiences with their students. Our approach is not a comprehensive educational tool and by necessity must be complemented by other teaching and processing tools.

We build on the proposition laid down in the early 20th century by John Dewey: People can construct knowledge through their own experience. Dewey had a significant impact on education as an advocate of learning through experience and practical experimentation. He established a different lens through which educators might view their teaching choices:

"... to imposition from above is opposed free activity; to learning from texts and teachers, learning through experience; to acquisition of isolated skills and techniques by drill is opposed acquisition of them as means of attaining ends which make direct vital appeal; to preparation for a more of less remote future is opposed making the most of the opportunities to present life; to static aims and materials is opposed acquaintance with a changing world ..." (Dewey, 1938, p. 19)

We are interested in how the experience of life gets translated into learning. Why do some people permanently change their outlook on life after experiencing an outdoor challenge, while others quickly return to their same habits and beliefs?

These variables occur because the learning that results from experience is often unstructured. For example, people may draw different conclusions from getting their first speeding ticket. For one it is a lesson in safer, more controlled driving.

For another it is further proof that crying doesn't work nearly as well as reputed. For a third person, the experience never enters long-term memory and little of it is actually stored. The complex arrangement of brain neurochemistry, genetics, emotional state, prior experience, and other influences combine in each moment to create learning.

What are some of the things we do know about how we learn?
Understanding how people learn turns out to be an incredibly difficult challenge. The actual path of acquiring new knowledge touches on many different places in the brain depending on the content and context of the learning. Only a few aspects of the process seem clear:

• Learning begins before consciousness and is ongoing in people with normal brain function.
• People learn the most when they want to learn.
• People learn from experience.
• People learn from conceptual forms and ideas.
• There are stages of cognitive and emotional development, and these are loosely related to learning.

(Brookfield, 1986, p. 25-30)

The Science of the Brain

Brain research in the last 20 years has exploded many of our previously held notions of how the brain works. Most importantly, we have learned that, throughout our lives, we are creating new brain cells. The brain is highly adaptable even at advanced ages, suggesting that old dogs can, in fact, learn new tricks. This is not to say that adult learning is easy. Beyond the age of 12, the brain is not creating connections quite as rapidly as it did before. Acquiring new knowledge becomes a slightly more difficult task. A review of what happens as the brain develops will help shed light on how we can use an understanding of brain neurochemistry to help groups we work with learn more effectively.

We are born with somewhere around two hundred billion neurons. Rather than being a blank slate upon which the world will write a personality, these neurons represent a sort of cumulative possibility function, the components of which include genes, fetal environment, nourishment, and the mother's emotional state. During the first few years of life, experience helps connect these neurons to each other. Those that are used and connected join together rapidly while those that are not used eventually fall away.

By about age three, we have cut our original gift of neurons in half to about 100 billion. At this point, "a kind of irreversibility sets in. There is this shaping process that goes on early, and then at the end of this process, be that age two, three or four, you have essentially designed a brain that probably is not going to change very much more" (Kotulak, 1996, p. 7). At this point those remaining 100 billion neurons have made an average of 10,000 connections. The connected neurons are able to form neural pathways that represent learning and memory. Our brains are able to ask and answer questions like, "What is an orange? What happens when I throw it? What did the last orange I ate taste like?"

Interestingly, these neural connections don't just wait around. The brain must be constantly exposed to new and different experiences. "Unless the brain is continuously challenged, it loses some of the connections that grew out of a college experience. The brains of university graduates who led mentally inactive lives had fewer connections than those of graduates who never stopped letting the light in" (Kotulak, 1996, p. 18).

How Does the Brain Learn?

The brain learns by taking in sensory data and then labeling, categorizing, and connecting that data to previously stored information. In the broadest sense, the brain learns everything through experience. The more neural connections are reinforced through repeated experience and multisensory stimulation, the greater the likelihood the information will be retained.

Confucius knew what modern MRI scans now confirm: "Tell me and I'll forget; show me and I'll understand; involve me and I'll remember." This correlates with the work done in the 1960's by the National Training Laboratories of Bethel, Maine (now the NTL Institute of Alexandria, Virginia). They studied the percentage of new learning that students retained after 24 hours of being taught by a particular teaching method. Their data showed that after lecture and reading techniques, students retained only 5% and 10% of the new information. By contrast, when the technique used was practice by doing or teaching others, the retention rate shot up to 75% and 90% respectively (Sousa, p. 95).

Using What We Know

We know that we should make experience multisensory, and we should encourage reflection and conscious processing of information. The challenge then is to use this information moment by moment in a debriefing process.

Jean Piaget offers an excellent starting place for understanding what we do with new information. Piaget developed the concepts of assimilation and accommodation. These are the processes that, stated simply, involve learning from either external stimuli or from internal thought processes.

Accommodation occurs when we adapt our view of the world to new sensory information. We see something new. This new experience is brought into the set of information that we previously held, and we adjust our internal notions to accommodate this new information.

Assimilation occurs when new stimulus fits into already established mental constructs. We experience a beautiful sunrise and file it into the mental category of beautiful experiences. We assimilate this new experience into an already existing set of beliefs.

As experiential facilitators, we can imagine a group struggling to place their experience. They alternate through different aspects of assimilating this experience into connections already established and accommodating their beliefs to make room for this new data. When we, as facilitators, understand this process, we can ask questions and offer support as they assimilate and accommodate.

Stages to Learning

David Kolb wrote one of the basic experiential learning texts, *Experiential Learning*, in 1984. Kolb noted the ways in which we grasp sensory data and transform it into knowledge. He combined the experiential philosophy of John Dewey, the cognitive developmental psychology of Jean Piaget, and the social psychology and action research contributions of Kurt Lewin to create a model of learning. Kolb spoke of four learning paradigms or stages (see figure 1). Each stage is related to the others, and all are necessary for learning that is important, long-lasting, and meaningful.

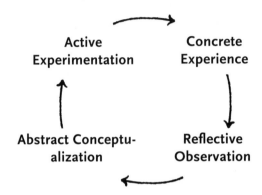

Figure 1: Kolb Theory of Experiential Learning

Kolb argued that different individuals process information and learn in terms of a dominant tendency in one of the above stages. For Kolb, these were not necessarily linear stages in a learning process, but rather, connected processes that individuals may or may not use to learn.

How can we use this understanding of learning to help develop and facilitate learning experiences? When you have this knowledge, you can guide your group to their own "aha" moments. "Aha" moments are the moments teachers live for. They happen when someone finally begins to put the pieces of a lesson together and molds them into a comprehensive understanding or belief that then becomes a part of their lives.

Micah experienced such a moment when conducting a Link Crew orientation where the seniors and juniors were serving as mentors/facilitators for the incoming freshmen. At one point, the mentors took their groups on a tour of the campus. Micah stopped into the restroom to wash his hands when a freshman boy came running in. Taking no notice of Micah, the boy began to fill up a water gun. Micah had specifically asked the leaders not to use water guns on their tour, so he suspected that this freshman was out to cause a little trouble.

Rather than take a traditional command-and-control approach, Micah tried to create a learning opportunity with the following conversation.

> Micah: Hey, what's going on?
> Freshman: (swiftly hiding gun) Uh, nothing.
> Micah: What are you doing with the water gun?
> Freshman: (gun hanging down at his side) Uh, nothing ... oh, my leader asked me to fill this up.
> Micah: Wow, you've only known me for a few moments and you may have already lied to me. How does that feel?
> Freshman: What?
> Micah: I asked the leaders not to use water guns, so it is possible that you are lying to me. Why did you do that?
> Freshman: Uh, I don't know.
> Micah: Is that something you do all the time? Lie to people you just met?
> Freshman: Well, no. I mean, I guess. Uh, am I in trouble?
> Micah: What do you think should happen now?
> Freshman: I guess I should give you the gun, right?
> Micah: Sure, if you think that's the right thing to do. What would you do differently next time?

> Freshman: Well, I guess I should stay with my group.
> Micah: Okay, sounds good.

Micah kept asking the boy questions that might get him to reflect on his actions. It was Micah's hope that as the boy reflected on his concrete experiences, he might begin to understand more productive ways of behaving and come to his own answers – experience his own "aha."

Of course this situation is not quite the same as a facilitator with a group. Micah represented an authority figure and the boy just wanted to get out of the way as quickly and painlessly as possible. Still, what might he have thought or learned if Micah had simply said, "Hey, you're not supposed to have water guns; hand it over!"

Constructivism

The model of learning just described is often associated with a constructivist paradigm. The constructivist school of thought has a rich tradition, and like any school of thought it is not without critique. Critics claim that this theory places too much emphasis on the cognitive processes, ignores subconscious and psychic ways of learning, and places emphasis on the individual and de-emphasis on the cultural and contextual aspects of learning.

- **What is learning from a constructivist point of view?** Essentially individuals are constantly constructing knowledge based on their experience of the world. Constructivism asserts that an individual's interactions with his/her environment produce specific observations which are then interpreted and generalized into concepts of the way the world works. These concepts are then called knowledge and used in future settings to guide behavior and feeling. This cycle then repeats as new experiences yield new observations which are furthered processed into new ideas for application.

You've Got a Stage, I've Got a Question

There have been many before us who proposed a cycle of questions to promote learning. Both of us were initially introduced to a form of questioning that roughly follows the Pfeiffer and Jones 5 Stage model (see figure 2). However, like other highly conceptual models, the Pfeiffer and Jones model is difficult for some to understand and challenging to master in a short period of time.

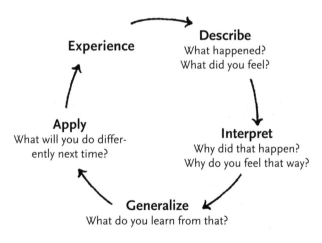

Figure 2: Adapted Pfeiffer and Jones 5 Stage Model

The simplicity of Outward Bound's "What? So What? Now What?" and James Neill's "Do, Review, Plan" is appealing, but it is difficult to achieve a consistent application of the process by a variety of facilitators. Although they are easy to remember, the challenge remains of really addressing each learning stage involved in processing the experience. Often simple models fail to adequately address what we see as the critical interpretation stage (i.e., asking "What?" then "Why?" before moving to "So What?").

"Follow-up" questions are another approach to facilitating experience. These are a list of specific questions related to the activity. Participants generally either connect directly to the questions and you have a successful discussion, or more commonly, a deafening silence follows as you work to make the group think about the specific issues raised by the question. These issues may or may not resonate with their experience. Practically, it is also awkward to hold a list of questions in your hand as you facilitate.

How The 5 Questions Model Fits In

The 5 Questions model rests on the foundation of brain research, stage theory of learning, and a constructivist paradigm. That's the theory behind the model. We want you to know this because the simplicity of each question is at first deceptive! And to be the most effective facilitator you can be, we want you to have all the background you can. Before we proceed, there are two more ideas to consider about learning: framing the experience and emotional stake.

Framing the Experience

The philosophy of The 5 Questions model is one of being "open to outcome," which is to be open to the learning that can emerge from the individuals and the group. This does not preclude having learning objectives. In every learning situation, a good facilitator will always be thinking about the objectives of the experience. You might even have possible learning scenarios in mind. For example, when teaching a lesson on the Civil War, you may want students to learn about specific economic factors that provided the subtext for the conflict around slavery. In a work group low ropes course, a facilitator may hope that colleagues face some of their conflicting behaviors and maybe even come to see that they can successfully overcome them. You are not at cross purposes with being open to outcome if you come into the learning environment with objectives that center around your hopes for the experience at hand. These objectives help the participants frame their experience.

How do you successfully frame an experience and remain open? Your objectives should focus on the process rather than the content. This means concerning yourself with *how* the group learns and the quality of the learning environment. It does not mean deciding exactly *what* the group will learn. In fact, it means most likely not knowing what the group will learn but remaining open to what that learning could be.

How then can your objectives best be achieved? Focus on keeping objectives behavioral and cognitive in scope rather than content-directed. For example, if you are doing a workshop on diversity, rather than orient yourself toward a particular leaning, i.e., "We are a judgmental species and participants must change their own internal stereotypes," focus instead on the quality of the experience, i.e., "Participants will have the opportunity to look closely at their own biases and engage in an honest dialogue about them."

The Notion of Stake

So the experience went really well and yet it seems that people still learned nothing. This dilemma brings us to yet another point on the nature of learning – the notion of "stake."

- **What is stake?** Think of it as the emotional or cognitive risk that participants feel. In general, the more emotional stake invested in the experience, the more powerful the learning opportunity. This is not to say that if you have nothing at stake you can't learn anything. Sometimes powerful learning can happen simply by watching from the sidelines; however, the potential of actually being in the game and having something to lose makes learning much more probable.

Imagine attending a retreat with a group of relative strangers. The facilitator asks for volunteers to demonstrate an important concept and, being adventurous, you raise your hand and step forward. How much do you have at risk in this moment? What if we replace the group of strangers with your closest friends? What about work colleagues? How does your thinking about participating in this experiment change based on who is observing?

Now, imagine the experiment involves hypnosis. The facilitator makes no mention of what kinds of activities you are going to undergo. Are you nervous yet? Some people might not be if they feel safe in the situation or maybe have a limited fear of embarrassment. For others, their hearts are starting to beat faster just reading about it. As your emotional stake rises, the possibility for a long-term "learning" increases. Interestingly, as you might no doubt imagine, we tend to learn more from extreme negative experiences than we do from extreme positive ones. If the facilitator were to proceed and embarrass you, many people might decide then and there never to volunteer again. Others might begin to establish parameters for their participation. Compare that with the person who felt minimal emotional stake in the experience. Embarrassed or not, they are unlikely to change their behavior in the future. They simply carry on as before.

It's Just a Game

If you work with young people, you have probably heard "this is just a game" a million times. They believe that because this is just a game they don't have to care about it, and their behavior ultimately doesn't matter. This is the game they are playing with themselves so they won't have to learn anything. They are saying to themselves, "If it is just a game to me, then I have no stake in the outcome and I don't need to reflect on what I said or did." As a facilitator with any group, you can raise the stakes involved simply by helping people see that they are always somewhat at risk.

Micah was doing a simulation that helps highlight experiences in win-win or win-lose situations with a group in Southern California. People have the opportunity to lie or cheat to win, and many groups opt for those behaviors. With Micah's particular group a lot of lying and cheating had gone on, which enabled one team to win "the game" easily. When the other group brought this up, the winning group smiled and said, "It doesn't matter if we lied; this was just a game and the point was to win, which we did." They didn't feel enough personal, emotional involvement in the experience to allow learning to occur.

Micah asked them to reflect on themselves in and out of the experience. "Do you typically lie or cheat in your lives? When do you find that helpful? When does it hurt? When did you decide it was okay to do so in this experience? Did you stop being yourselves while you were playing today? Did you become someone else?" Micah raised the stakes by having them look closer and acknowledge accountability for their behavior. His questions allowed the group to look at their own patterns of interaction and ultimately at the patterns at work in the world around them. When you raise the stakes, you increase the potential for learning.

Too Much at Stake

There is the potential to raise the stakes too high in a simulated environment. Just like having nothing at stake, when participants have too much at stake they are also at risk of shutting themselves off to learning and moving instead into a survival mode. This can happen when individuals are singled out in an unsupportive environment. A "fight or flight" instinct engages, and extreme resistance can quickly build up. This creates blocks to learning that are impossible to overcome. When this is the situation, it is best to lower the stakes. Look for ways to take the focus away from particular individuals and ask questions that are potentially less threatening. It doesn't serve the group or the facilitator to force learning into a situation that is not ready for it.

Getting It Just Right

In the end it is a balancing act. Figure 3 shows the balance between not enough and too much at stake. There is a fine line between not enough and too much emotional or cognitive investment for an environment to lend itself to learning experiences. Facilitators stand a better chance of creating incredible learning opportunities when focusing on some of the fundamentals of effective facilitation like creating a supportive and productive environment, encouraging supportive and reflective dialogue, and checking your own agenda at the door.

Figure 3

Putting It All Together

Understanding how learning occurs and what enhances or hinders learning will make you a better facilitator. As you think about your role in the group, you can draw on the concepts of a learning cycle, brain-based learning, learning objectives, and emotional stake to set up a framework for how you might philosophically approach your task. We constantly learn more on these topics. Participants, colleagues, and our own experiences of being facilitated continue to provide a practical backdrop to the theories we hold to be true. Ultimately, a theory is only as good as its ability to provide useful explanation and prediction of actual occurrence. Additionally, theory alone is rarely useful. Part of the motivation for writing this book was a belief that we could make practical some of the theoretical underpinnings of debriefing experiences. The next few chapters aim to do just that.

Chapter Two | Creating Space & the Facilitator Mind-Set

"IN TEACHING, IT IS THE METHOD AND NOT THE CONTENT
THAT IS THE MESSAGE ... THE DRAWING OUT,
NOT THE PUMPING IN." —Ashley Montague

When a group gathers for the purpose of learning from a shared experience, it is common and often helpful for someone to step into the role of facilitator. In this context, the facilitator's role is to guide the group and the group members to their own learning. Contrast this with the job of a teacher, whose job is to guide students to a defined set of learning. A facilitator presupposes that the group will have all the answers. The job of the facilitator is to make the process easier. That's not to say the process will be easy every step of the way, as it often is not. It does mean that it is the task of the facilitator to tend to the process.

This chapter describes the most important things to consider before you begin asking questions of the group and debriefing the experience. When facilitators pay attention to these items and adopt these mental mind-sets, group members consistently go deeper into their own profound learning. There are wonderful resources for learning to facilitate, many of which are listed in our references. This chapter is meant to highlight the most compelling and practical aspects of creating space and getting into a helpful mind-set for facilitation.

Creating Space

Imagine that physical space is a real entity. It can help or hurt. It can make the group more or less comfortable. It is *part* of the group and the experience. You can and should tend to the physical space as it will dramatically impact your success. Once you make the mental shift to believe this concept, it will be difficult not to notice the quality of the spaces in which you find yourself. "How will people feel in this space? How will it protect or create comfort for the inhabitants? How will the space support the activity that will be done in this room?" As an architect uses windows, doors, and walls to affect the room, facilitators move furniture and arrange bodies in order to impact the experience of the conversation that will take place.

Working predominantly in schools, we have had our share of challenging spaces. We have conducted trainings in libraries and cafeterias, on football fields and in science labs. Every time we walk into a new space we try to imagine the group interacting within the space. Where will everyone sit? What distractions are present? What might get in the way? Do everything you can to rearrange the room to suit your purposes. As a facilitator, you must imagine that you manage the space and give yourself permission to construct it in a way that will work for you.

Ideally, a group will reflect in the same space used to conduct the experience. If the space itself is too distracting, then the closest appropriate space will have to work.

- **What would be the best setup for group reflection?** The space should be large enough to accommodate all group members seated in a circle with no furniture or other items in the middle of the circle. If the group will be talking for a while, it is helpful for everyone to have a comfortable chair. Or, if the group is flexible enough, group members could sit comfortably on the floor or ground. When seated, everyone should be able to see everyone else. The facilitator should be part of the circle at the same physical level as the participants (i.e., everyone seated or everyone standing).

Where you position yourself indicates a power relationship. Teachers stand in front of the class. Colleagues gather around a table. Leaders sit at the head of the table. Friends sit with each other. Where do you put yourself? If you stand up in front, you have immediately created some physical separation between you and the group.

Mari watched a high school student lead a group of her peers through a debriefing. The student stood up front as she imagined a leader should. The group sat scattered in desks as she attempted to get them to answer her debriefing questions. The group largely ignored her. Later the student leader commented that her group "sucked." Mari asked her to reflect on how she had positioned herself relative to the rest of the group. Slowly she came to understand the power of levels and seating. Such a simple thing, yet it can make or break an experience.

Additional things to consider when creating the space:

- What interruptions might occur and how will they be handled?
- Where is the bathroom, so you can tell participants?
- Will people be coming in once you've started? How will you welcome them into the conversation?
- Is the temperature in the room or outside where you are sitting not too hot and not too cold?
- Can everyone hear everyone else?
- Are there any random, annoying noises or visuals that will distract group members? If so, can you adjust things so there are no such noises or visuals?

Write these down to create your own checklist. Refer to your list as you walk into your next facilitation experience to create better opportunities for success.

To move from the space where the experience happened to the space where reflection will occur, it is important for the facilitator to create that new space swiftly and with as much flow as possible so that group members don't even notice you're tending to the space. This means, if at all possible, consider the physical space before the experience occurs. Move the furniture and adjust the temperature before people arrive. Have a plan for breaks. Make sure the space is appropriate for the size of your group. If *you* think about it, then they won't have to; their attention can be on the conversation and the learning.

The Power of a Circle

Forming a circle is the most ancient and powerful way for a group to symbolically be in an egalitarian relationship to one another. Making time to form a circle is well worth the effort because conversation flows more easily when everyone is at the same physical level and can see everyone else. Circles by their very nature invite everyone to participate. A circle helps bring the shy or quiet ones into the process and, since there is no stage, it tends to calm the loud and showy ones. In a circle, the facilitator can more easily guide the process.

Some groups may resist forming a circle. It could be because they don't want to be that intimate with one another, and circles are intimate. Or perhaps they don't want to be held accountable to one another. Another common reason groups won't easily move into a circle is they just don't have much practice at it. In any of these circumstances, it's best to use a little humor and grace while simply insisting upon and expecting cooperation. If you have chairs, it will help to have them placed in a circle.

While facilitating a group of school administrators, Mari had one particularly intransigent participant. This person chose a chair several feet away from the circle and turned slightly, as if to physically indicate his unwillingness to join the conversation as an equal. Mari gathered the rest of the group and quietly whispered instructions. The group simultaneously picked up their chairs and moved to form a circle that included this gentleman. He sat there stunned. As the group took their seats, never saying a word directly to him, he finally laughed and said, "Okay, okay, I get it." He then turned his chair in and became a willing and valuable contributor to the conversation. Over and over we have seen that circling the group together from the beginning makes an incredible difference. Sometimes gentle nudging is required.

The Facilitator Mindset – Genuine Curiosity

As the facilitator, you are acting as a conduit for the group; therefore, your internal mindset has a definite impact on them. If there is nothing else you can remember or do as a facilitator, show genuine curiosity about the participants and their experience, and profound learning will emerge.

How would you define the word "genuine"? Synonyms for genuine are authentic, real, true. It is not fake, false, or imitation. Think of someone you know who is genuine and likely you will smile and feel a heart connection. That is the power of genuine.

We have seen a number of people facilitate the way they think they are supposed to – using the right words and gestures. Still somehow they seem not themselves. It is like they are playing the role of "facilitator" rather than being genuinely curious. How can you find the person within you that is not wearing any masks? Who are you? How do you bring that person to your facilitation?

Now consider the definition of "curiosity." To wonder, to explore, to be engaged, to feel your mind awake: This is curiosity. When was the last time you were passionately curious? Can you remember a time when you were so curious that questions kept rumbling in your mind? What sparked that curiosity? How did you feed it?

How do you combine the two concepts? Really think about the two together; let yourself be genuinely curious about the members of the group with whom you will work. Where have they come from? What does this experience mean for them? What possibilities exist?

To help invoke a state of genuine curiosity, remember when you were 5 years old or think of a 5-year-old you know. Recall the intense curiosity and interest in the world they have. Put yourself in the vortex of that curiosity. When that 5-year-old asks a question, their entire being seeks the answer, and when the answer comes, another question immediately arises. The questions and answers tumble together in the delight of discovery. As a facilitator, your challenge is to call forth that state of delight and curiosity in yourself.

Lessons From Improv Comedy

In addition to genuine curiosity, we have found three concepts from the world of improvisational comedy or improv to be invaluable for remaining open to outcome when facilitating a group reflection.

- **What is improv?** It is a form of theatre in which the actors, known as players, act within a given format. Because they are only given an outline or a set of rules, all the words and movements are not practiced in advance. They must improvise in the moment. This is akin to what facilitators of experiential activities do. There is a structure, but we never know *exactly* what we will need to do or say. As prepared as you may be, every group brings something different to the experience.

All excellent improv players operate from three intertwined beliefs about the process, their fellow players, the audience, and the set. They are **yes/and**, **go big**, and **total support**.

We have borrowed these concepts and lay no claim to having created them. Both of us have studied improv in a variety of settings, and we have deep appreciation for professional improv players. We are not them. What we have done with great success is to take the principles of improv and adapt them to help new facilitators become increasingly skilled. By thinking and playing with these three concepts, facilitation students have generated powerful insights. Each of these beliefs runs counter in some way to the general cultural milieu. They require some level of careful study and are helped by constant reinforcement.

Yes/And

The goal of each improv player, and in our case each facilitator, is to keep the scene engaging and moving forward. Therefore, players build on and contribute to what has happened in the scene, taking the storyline in a new and creative direction. In facilitation, this means that the facilitator builds on, probes for depth, and encourages group members to inquire from themselves and fellow group members about what is being discussed.

What does an engaging environment look like. Recall those times when you have been with friends or colleagues and it seemed as if every idea built on those that came before. Although not every idea is acted on or even seen as good, every idea seems to have a place because it helps lead to the next one. And the next one might be brilliant.

How does yes/and change the group's response? The opposite of **yes/and** is **no/but** or **yes/but**. Think of a time when you enthusiastically shared an idea with someone who responded with "That's a great idea, but what about ...?" The "but" in the response has the effect of letting the air out of your enthusiasm balloon. In improv, that's known as a block. The person with the idea has to use extra energy to overcome the block, energy that could be used to be more creative and since it's comedy, more funny. In life, when we hear "**yes, but** ...," it deflates us. We have to use extra energy to overcome the block and re-inflate – energy that could be more productively used in getting to the next brilliant idea.

When we deliberately change our language to **yes/and** and really mean it, people open up and get more into their ideas. Notice the subtle and powerful shift in this response to your enthusiasm and your idea: "That's a great idea, and what about also doing ...." **Yes/and** opens up the pathway to synergy and tremendous potential.

Look at the following dialogue as an example:

Jeff: I wish we had more instructions before we played. I felt like you didn't tell us what we were doing so we didn't really have a chance to succeed!

Facilitator: Yes, and what did you do with the instructions that I did give?

Jeff: Well, we tried to understand them, but we wasted a lot of time wondering what we could and could not do. It was never made clear.

Facilitator: Yes, and do you think it is interesting that you wasted so much time?

One way to think about **yes/and** is to break it down. "Yes" refers to acknowledgment – not necessarily agreement – that what someone said was true for them in that moment. It is a way of saying, "Yes, you did just say that." This lets the person know they were heard rather than immediately dismissed. Starting the sentence with "but" or "no" is a denial of what they said and can lead some to believe that they were not truly heard in the first place.

"And" is additive; it moves the conversation forward by adding what is true or unique for you. For instance, a friend wants to see a movie but you are hungry. Rather than shutting down your friend, you can acknowledge his/her desire and then add your perspective: "Yes, and it would be great to get something to eat, because I'm really hungry right now." "And" enables you to have a place in the conversation and to keep it moving forward without having to simply agree with what others are saying.

Yes/and is more about a mind-set than the actual language. You can easily **no/but** someone with the words **yes/and**. Look at the following dialogue:

Calvin: I was thinking that as a group we should have taken some time to plan more at the beginning.

Angela: Yes, and that is exactly what you always say!

In this example, Angela uses the words **yes/and**, but her meaning and intention is still to put up a block for Calvin. To really understand the spirit of acknowledgment and addition takes some practice.

How can you use **yes/and** when someone makes a racial slur or publicly demeans another group member? These can be some of the most powerful moments for a group and must be handled carefully. Think of how different responses will impact the group. A comment like, "It is not appropriate to say things like that in this group," is certainly understandable and sometimes advisable and has a very specific reaction. It shuts down further communication. This may not always be the right choice. What might happen if you simply answered, "Yes, and how is it that you have come to believe such a hurtful thing?" Still laden with judgment, this sentence allows for a continuation of the dialogue. Even less judgmental would be a simple question: "Yes, and why do you believe that?" Whatever your style, holding to the concept of **yes/and**, even when it is difficult, can be transformative for the group and also for you.

- **How do you keep "yes/and" in the front of your mind?** The **first** technique is simply to write in big letters, on whatever notes you may use, "YES, AND." Simply seeing the words as you facilitate calls to mind the belief. The **second** technique is to stay constantly aware of your own emotional state. If you feel yourself tightening and resisting a group or a particular person's energy, mentally go through a process of what would happen if you could say **yes/and** to this person. How might you work with them differently if you didn't try so hard to resist?

Go Big

The idea of **go big** is to show up fully in your being and in your presence with the group. For an improv player, it means to move past the fear of doing or saying the wrong thing, and instead trust the dynamic flow of the scene. For a facilitator, it means to be fully present with the group and trust the process and your skills as a facilitator. To both an improv player and a facilitator it means daring to be outrageous or quiet and trusting that what you say and do will be the right thing, and if it isn't, even that will be the right thing.

It is also important to consider what **go big** is not. It is not monopolizing the conversation. It is not jumping around and being a cheerleader. **Go big** is not about upstaging your group or giving them the answers.

Go big means to be alert and aware with every cell of your mental and physical being. Refuse to be small. Say "no" to the parts of you that critique and judge and second guess. The world is already in too much pain for any of us to act small. What you do makes a difference for others. **Go big** says that the difference you make will be a big one. Use your skills and talents to the maximum of your ability. Do not let any person or group convince you that you are small. As Nelson Mandela so eloquently quoted Maryanne Williamson, "Our deepest fear is not that we are inadequate. Our deepest fear is that we are powerful beyond measure."

The power of adopting a **go big** mind-set is that it enables you to take risks. You can go where the group needs you to go and say what the group needs you to say. Actors refer to this as "committing" to the moment. In a facilitation moment this might mean calling out a particular behavior.

Mari was facilitating a group of high school students through a low ropes set of initiatives. The group was generally not engaging at their highest potential. At one point, a student commented that they were tired of playing these stupid games. Mari's heart sank; the students had been negative all day and she was tired. She sat quietly for a minute and then decided to **go big**. Mari looked directly at the student and quietly responded, "Do you notice that you are constantly playing games?" For some reason this was the right question to ask. The whole group got serious for the first time. They thought deeply about the kinds of games people play with others and with themselves. Not only was it a profound conversation, but the entire group became much more interactive. Looking back, it may not seem like a great risk. However, in that moment, Mari knew she was going big.

- **Can you go big and not get your ego wrapped up in your success?**
- **Can you go big and say nothing at all? Can you go big and have**
- **the ability to acknowledge that the next time you can do it even**
- **better? Go big** holds two things as true: **First**, you are capable
- of being there for your group in a way that will manifest profound
- change. **Second**, it is not entirely about you. Holding both these
- beliefs at the same time can make your facilitation ascend to a
- more powerful level.

Total Support

Total support means standing with your people. It is the mind-set that exclaims, "I am here for you!" In improv, **total support** means moving through a scene in such a way that each player looks as good as possible. If one player is center stage, the other players move and behave in ways that make the focal person look as good as possible.

Very clearly **total support** means never demeaning, belittling, or humiliating someone in the group. For some of us, the temptation to be negatively sarcastic or to put people "in their place" rises up easily. How can you support a group and dismiss them at the same time? You can't.

What does it mean to facilitate with total support? Extend a strong, permeating energy of support through everything: yourself, the group, what is being said, where the conversation is heading. Believe in what is happening, and support the people and the conversation. Look out for everyone all at once and with equal attention. When you operate from this place, group members will begin to feel **total support**. As **total support** builds in a group, people begin to trust themselves and one another, resulting in more creativity, depth, and risk taking.

An important note: **Total support** does not mean surrendering yourself because an important part of **total support** is supporting yourself, too. You cannot allow yourself to be demeaned or belittled by the group any more than you would allow group members to do that to each other. You are not supporting the group or yourself by letting one participant dominate the debrief.

The Challenges of Total Support
Facilitators constantly struggle with when to move a conversation forward. People like to rehash moments and ideas. A comment that stirs several people to want to contribute is tough to move away from. Even when the group does move away from a topic, some participants demand to move backward so that their perspectives can be heard. You don't have to facilitate long to understand that groups can cycle. Many facilitators feel they have to ensure that every person is heard. The question to ask is whether allowing everyone to be heard on every topic is really supporting the group as a whole.

How can you be in **total support** of yourself, the group, and the individuals all at the same time? Our cultural biases are dramatically evident here. Part of being in a relativistic, politically correct culture is that we have an intense focus on and respect for the individual. This is wonderful as long as we also acknowledge that groups have needs as well. Sometimes supporting one individual by letting him/her talk on and on is actively not supporting the group as a whole. Sometimes you simply need to move on.

Micah experienced an excellent example of **total support**. After a Link Crew training program, where high school seniors and juniors served as facilitators for incoming freshmen, Micah asked the upper-class leaders about their experience. One senior said that her small group of freshmen had started out being very uncooperative and difficult. Micah asked what she had done to get through her sessions. She said that about halfway through she stopped using the curriculum and just ask the freshmen to tell her what they were looking forward to in high school. The kids were excited to tell this senior some of the things they were looking forward to. She listened closely to what they were interested in and then asked if they would like some more information that might help them be successful. At this point she dove back into the curriculum, now with a group that was enthusiastic and interested. Her support of their dreams for high school enabled her to support them with some immediate information they needed. Essentially, she was able to support where they were in the moment while not losing sight of where they needed to be.

There are times when the group process or conversation is not going the way you thought it would or should. Perhaps it has taken a particularly harmful turn and doesn't seem to be a productive conversation any longer. One solution is to breathe into what is happening, step back mentally, and let go. Think **total support** and see if the conversation shifts. See if you can find the wisdom that is trying to emerge from the group. Trust it, trust yourself, and trust the group.

You may need to push the group or individuals past their stuck places. **Total support** means to let everyone's self-worth and participatory ability remain intact while you ask the tough questions. Make the effort to include and, at the same time, move the process and conversation. Keep in mind that **total support** applies to all levels of the group interaction as well as to you. As we grow in our ability to facilitate conversation, we also grow in our ability to hold together the multiple contradictions of **total support**.

All of these **yes/and**, **go big**, and **total support** are mental models for facilitators to keep in mind when working with a group. They should deeply influence the decisions you make as you guide a group to its own wisdom and learning.

Check the Baggage at the Door

To some extent, facilitators cannot avoid bringing their own issues into the process. Notice that nowhere in this book do we claim that a facilitator must be neutral. Although neutrality is certainly a worthy goal in many settings, it is next to impossible. Your life experience, values, beliefs, and habits will intercede despite your best efforts. It is important, however, for the facilitator to have a clear and present mind-set because his/her level of distraction will impact the group and the group process.

- **Facilitation must incorporate the best of what you are.** Your power and passion, your potential must be available to your group as you guide them toward understanding. The real challenge is to bring only those pieces of you that move the group forward. Leave your negative attitudes, distractions, and prejudices behind. We call this process "getting clear." There are many ways to get clear, the following is one example.

- **Clearing Protocol:** (Allow about 3 to 5 minutes.) Breathe in and out slowly. As you do so, feel every part of your body. Move from your toes to your head. Be sure to give extra attention to your **gut** (for following your intuition), your **hands** (for guiding the group), and your **heart** (for sensing what has heart and meaning). As you breathe in, imagine yourself alive and full and ready for anything. As you exhale, let go and relax into trust and support. Let go of all distractions. Feel energy and focus from every part of your being. Smile inside and outside.

In the End, It's About Being Open to Outcome

Recently, we watched an otherwise talented facilitator throw away a great debriefing opportunity. The facilitator was set on having the group notice how they had broken the rules established in the setup to the activity. He was so blinded by this prejudice for learning within the activity that he completely missed several participants who wanted to talk about other aspects of the experience. A facilitator can do an initiative so many times that s/he may have a preconceived expectation of what the participants "should" learn. The challenge is to adapt the "beginner's mind" referred to in Zen. Each time, try to experience and debrief an activity with the fresh enthusiasm of the first time you played and processed.

No matter how valuable, how real and present in the experience, how useful in life a set of learning might be, if the participants don't arrive at the understanding in their own fashion, it is unlikely that the learning will stick. The intention of experiential learning is to help participants get more connected to their own source of learning and knowing. The answers are no more in you as a facilitator than they are in a book or lecture. For the group, the answers must come from within.

Chapter Three | The 5 Questions

"IF YOU'RE LUCKY, YOU WON'T FIND WHAT YOU'RE
LOOKING FOR." —Varekai, Cirque du Soliel

What Are They?

The 5 Questions embody a specific framework for debriefing an experience. They are a collective set of questions that for beginning facilitators can be used in order. For more advanced and experienced facilitators, they can be used as guideposts in facilitating a closure process. The 5 Questions are an attempt to take what we know about learning and present it in a "user-friendly" manner. The approach is based on the "learning cycle" as defined by Kolb and Pfeiffer and Jones and discussed in Chapter One.

Let's also say a few words about what The 5 Questions are not. They are not a comprehensive learning framework. They do not work every time with every group in every situation. They are a starting place and are not an ending place. For beginning facilitators, we created The 5 Questions to be an easy and practical starting place for debriefing conversations.

Once you know and have tried The 5 Questions, we believe you will benefit from exploring deeper and richer learning constructs such as those mentioned in Chapter One of this book. For experienced facilitators, we offer The 5 Questions as a framework from which to ask further questions as you guide participants through the learning cycle.

The 5 Questions have proven themselves extremely useful in and adaptable to a variety of settings. We have taught these questions to 14-year-olds who have been able to successfully use them with their peers. Teachers with more than 30 years of experience in the classroom have found them to be valuable tools to add to their repertoire. Experienced facilitators have found worth in both the simple approach and the insight into the study of asking questions. In turn, we benefit from the feedback of these practitioners. They have helped broaden our perspective and expand how we think about and use The 5 Questions.

The 5 Questions are:
1. Did you notice ... ?
2. Why did that happen?
3. Does that happen in life?
4. Why does that happen?
5. How can you use that?

The questions can be correlated to most learning cycle methodologies. We most often associate it to the Pfeiffer and Jones approach as seen in figure 1.

These questions are not random. They are the result of trial-and-error experimentation over hundreds of facilitation experiences. The questions each work together to make specific very general approaches to facilitating learning.

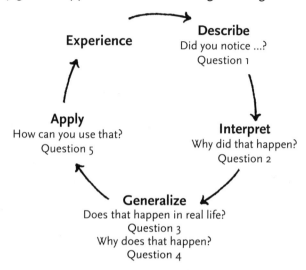

Figure 1: The 5 Questions applied to a 5 Stage Learning Cycle model

How Do They Work? Why Do They Work?
Following is an explanation of the purpose of each question in the process, which will give you a more comprehensive view of how and why this model works.

Question 1: Did You Notice ... ?
"Did you notice any fear as you were climbing?" "Did you notice how hesitant everyone seemed to be in taking the first step?" "Did you notice that a few people really took a leadership role?" "Did you notice how quickly you responded?"

The question "Did you notice ...?" is an attempt to get participants to look back at a specific observation made by the facilitator. The initial reaction of most people after a powerful experience is to want to talk about it; people naturally want to describe what happened to them and how it felt. "Did you notice ...?" allows participants to take part in a conversation about their experience. The facilitator is giving them permission to tell their story.

"Did you notice ... ?" is intentionally not an open-ended question and specifically requires a yes/no answer. Many advocate the use of open-ended questions to allow participants to describe their experience without bias. It is important, however, to note that Question 1 is definitely not, "What did you notice?" The "..." after "Did you notice" requires the facilitator to fill in the blank by carefully observing the group for powerful moments. The effect of the entire debriefing process can be determined from this seemingly insignificant question. The more a facilitator understands the power of this question, the better the facilitation experience.

Often, the opening question in a debriefing process does not provide for or create the space for powerful learning. It can, in fact, often be too big a question for the group to tackle first thing after an intensive experiential activity. In the best facilitative environment, participants would be able to cogently discuss their thoughts and feelings around an experience because they would have total recollection of it. They would be able to identify what they felt, saw, heard, touched, tasted, thought, and smelled. This is often hard for people to do, however, because rarely are we asked to describe, at any level of detail, something we just experienced. In most learning situations, this process of reflection happens at a subconscious level. In first asking an open-ended question such as "What just happened?" we've found many participants completely unable to describe their experience at any level of useful detail. When this is the case, the debriefing experience is in trouble from the very first question. Here is a possible scenario:

Facilitator: So what did you just experience?
Group: Silence.
Facilitator: Did anyone have any reactions to that experience?
Group: Silence.
Facilitator: Maria, what did you see happen in the group?
Maria: Uh, nothing.
Facilitator: So we just spent 30 minutes and you guys didn't notice anything?!

Several challenges are potentially at work here. The first is that it may seem that the facilitator has a particular agenda and the group doesn't know what that agenda may be. We are so used to "teachers" having the answers and asking us questions which are "rigged" that no one wants to say what s/he experienced for fear of being wrong.

The second challenge is that sometimes the group really doesn't know how to put their experience into words. Certainly they were conscious during it and are likely thinking about issues that came up for them, but some groups find it difficult to put those thoughts into words.

Third, some groups simply don't want to acknowledge that they care. They are doing their best to pretend that they are actually not present. In some groups and/or cultures, answering a question is a sign of emotional commitment that can be easily ridiculed. The rationale is, "If I answer this question, then it means I actually care, and if I care and no one else does, then I look foolish."

The last challenge is that sometimes participants really don't know what just happened, or they do know and feel badly about it, so they don't want to discuss it. Our friend Chellie, a middle school P.E. teacher in Colorado, hears the same thing every parent hears almost every day when calling a student on bad behavior: "Wha'd I do?" The truth is that the student is fully aware of what s/he did, but just doesn't want to own it. This can also be true of groups in the debriefing process, particularly groups that struggled or exhibited some questionable behavior during the activity. It is difficult for anyone to admit to less than stellar behavior, particularly in front of others. We predict that scientists will someday uncover the Denial Neuron, the brain cell bandit that sneaks off with particularly incriminating knowledge. Imagine how different corporate scandal hearings might be if there was actually scientific validation supporting a defendant's response of "I can not recollect that particular piece of information."

Each of these challenges requires a different and potentially nuanced response from a facilitator. The framing of Question 1, "Did you notice ...?" as a closed-ended question helps to meet each of these and other challenges head-on.

Question 1 launches us into the **describe/publish/concrete experience stage of learning**. The goal in this stage is to clearly identify what just happened. While many would argue that only an open-ended question will get you a meaningful response, we have found incredible success beginning debriefings with this closed-ended question.

- Starting with a facilitator-driven, **closed-ended question** offers at least two distinct advantages. **First**, it allows the facilitator to direct the initial focus of the conversation, thus creating the opportunity to have a somewhat directed conversation. While it is true that we advocate remaining open to the outcome of a debriefing, we also believe that giving the conversation a guided focus from the outset creates a solid foundation for the forthcoming discussion.

- The **second** advantage to using a closed-ended question is that this type of question is easier for participants to answer than an open-ended, broader question. This is especially helpful when you are working with a challenging group. When you ask, "Did you notice ...?" the participants can simply nod their heads in response; there really is no risk to them. Once they have nodded their heads, or said yes or no, they have engaged in the observation. More importantly, though, they have admitted to some level of knowledge. Now you have them. That initial commitment is often all it takes to hook them into a deeper level of reflection.

As you become more skilled as a facilitator, or work with groups that are more capable, it is perfectly fine to begin a group conversation with an open-ended question like "What did you notice?" Ultimately, choosing the type of question with which to begin your debrief comes down to an assessment of your facilitative abilities as well as your group's willingness to engage.

So, what do you notice? To make the first question work requires one critical skill: **observation**. Becoming a powerful observer ought to be a facilitator's first task. In every group experience there are literally innumerable issues that might be raised. Take the time to ask yourself what you are observing. Why did that piece of information rise to the top of the million other possibilities?

The **objective of observation** is to provide a mirror for participants to look into and to open up the possibility for learning from what they see. The things you notice as a facilitator guide your understanding and capability to help a group learn. Some things in every group experience are more worth noticing than others. Observing what a facilitator notices often says more about the facilitator than about the group's experience. As we observe our own observations, we gain the power to look inside the process of facilitation itself. Now that is paying attention!

Imagine a group playing an activity called Team Juggling. This initiative requires team members to work together to keep a certain number of objects in the air. For instance, the team might be randomly throwing four tennis balls around the circle with the intent of keeping all the balls moving and not having any one of the team members drop a ball.

As the facilitator, you notice that the team never stops the action to discuss possible strategies. They are simply having a great time throwing the balls at each other. Your first question might be, "Did you notice that you never stopped the action to discuss strategy?" This will launch the group into a reflection about strategy and planning. If, however, your first question is based on a different observation, the conversation could go in an entirely different direction. For example, "Did you notice that John consistently passed to Mario, and that Chelsea never got the ball?" This might send the group into a dialogue about skills and abilities as well as fairness and teamwork. Both issues were present at the same time in the group, as well as probably twenty other relevant issues. The question becomes, what are you as the facilitator trying to help the group look at?

The way you approach observation will inform the initial direction and focus of the debrief. Take a moment to consider the different questions you might ask yourself as a facilitator. For instance, you may take **a scientific approach** and look for some of the following data sets:

- How much time elapsed?
- Who contributed and how much?
- Was the objective reached?
- How many different strategies were tried?

By looking for data, you open up a frank conversation about what actually occurred. What can be measured and compared? You can focus the dialogue along the lines of what a group was attempting to achieve versus what was actually achieved.

Using **an anthropological approach** might mean observing by setting yourself up as an outsider, able to see the interaction of the group in ways that the group itself cannot. You might expand that to a more holistic approach and ask what you are not seeing that you should:

- Who had power in the group?
- How did they acquire that power?
- What rules did the group operate under?
- Which rules were followed? Which broken?
- What assumptions were made?

When you look at each group as a mini-society with their own customs and silent protocols, the worlds of culture and habit collide into a fascinating opportunity to provide new learning.

A third option is to take **a psychological approach**. We do not mean that you should attempt to solve individual pathologies but merely take the opportunity to look closely at individuals and their behaviors. The following questions might be appropriate:

- Why did she take a leadership role?
- Was anyone displaying strong emotions?
- How does he react to being consistently ignored?
- She seemed frustrated early on. How could you tell?
- Who was the most focused on completing the task?

Looking deeply at individuals and then raising possibilities with the group can often provide profound reflection.

As you can see, careful and creative observation is the key to asking the question that can open your group to reflection and focus their attention. Following up with Question 2 leads them further down the path of powerful learning possibilities.

Question 2: Why Did that Happen?

At this point in the debriefing process you have hopefully gained some ground with your group. With either a yes answer or a nod of the head, your group has admitted to noticing something about the activity you just did. An observational anchor has been established and that observation has had a chance to replay in the minds of the participants. Now it is time to search for the meaning behind that observation. What is the group's interpretation of what just happened?

Question 2 is associated with the **interpretation stage of learning**. A great number of learning cycle models leave this stage out entirely. In part this is because many adult groups interpret on their own, moving swiftly from describing their actions ("We worked well together") to interpreting their actions ("We worked so well because we have really gotten to know each other"). Although many individuals do this on their own, it is important for the facilitator to be able to keep track of whether an individual has actually interpreted and at what level. Sometimes facilitators want to skip quickly past asking for the group's interpretation of the activity and go directly to asking what the grouped learned and having them make other connections. That will only be successful if the group really understands the motivation, causation, or meaning behind the actions or feelings that they experienced.

Humans have searched for meaning longer than recorded history. As a species, it seems we are not content to just observe things. We search for explanations and then create our own interpretations for why things happen. This natural desire is to our advantage as facilitators. No matter how challenging the group, participants can barely resist trying to find meaning once they have committed to an observation. The more powerful and interesting the observation, the more hooked participants will be in the search for why it happened. A typical exchange might go as follows:

> Facilitator: Did you notice how long it took the group to develop a solution? (Question 1)
> Participant: Yes, it was really frustrating!
> Facilitator: Why did that happen? (Question 2)
> Participant: Well, we didn't understand the rules at first and then it took some time to figure out who was going to do what.

This question can work equally well whether the group did or did not notice the issue raised by the facilitator. The question just changes slightly from "Why did that happen?" to, "Why did you not notice?" The objective is simply to help the group move from the stage of reliving their experience through describing their actions and feelings, to one of interpreting those actions and feelings.

As a group struggles to make sense of their actions, behaviors, and feelings, there is one important pitfall to watch for: a lack of information, causing an inaccurate interpretation. Take a look at any population of adolescent children. They are continually struggling to make sense of the observations they are making and sometimes come up with amazing and all-encompassing rationalizations: "She doesn't like me because I don't have the right jeans!" "If you don't step on a crack, nothing bad will happen" (at least hopefully your mother's back will be safe – knock on wood). "I only got a bad grade because the teacher doesn't like me." The list can go on and on.

We, as adults, are not immune to inaccurate interpretation either. Consider the difficulty we often have in accepting responsibility for a mistake we have made. How easy is it to blame someone else? What about a friend who acts rudely to you one day? It's easy to immediately consider that he or she may not like you anymore when the case may be that she simply had just heard some bad news and was not in the mood to talk. On a more global scale, every day we can observe the personal conflict and societal discontent inspired by varied interpretations of either political or religious beliefs.

It is the accuracy with which we interpret that determines what we learn from any given event in our lives. This is true with debriefing activities as well. What do you do with a group or individual whose answers are not entirely accurate, either way off base, or slightly skewed? How do you help the group or individual come to the realization that there are other interpretations that could be more accurate and that could take them to a deeper level of learning? That is when you take the group to the next step and dig a little deeper using a form of Question 2.

- **Why did that *really* happen?** Two things are required to help your groups connect their observations to accurate interpretation. **First**, you must make sure you made a careful and accurate observation. When you ask, "Did you notice ...?" make sure that the group is really all on the same page with the observation. In other words, whether the response is yes or no, there has to be a commitment that they either did observe what you noticed, or a commitment that they did not observe it. Either answer is fine, but the commitment to observation is key.

Second, when you ask "Why did that happen?" listen closely. You are not listening for a particular "right answer;" you are listening for an answer that is accurate and connected.

Let's review a potential conversation:

> Facilitator: Did you notice that I was able to win every game? (Question 1)
> Participant: Yes. How did you do that?
> Facilitator: What do you think? Why did I win each time? (Question 2)
> Participant: You cheated!
> Facilitator: If I didn't cheat, why else do you think I won each time? (Question 2 – restated)
> Participant: You played before, you know the strategy.
> Facilitator: So you think I was able to win because I knew the strategy? (Reflection)
> Participant: Yes.

The facilitator began by highlighting the observation that she was able to win each time. Once the participants were anchored in the acknowledgment of the observation, the facilitator moved on to Question 2, "Why did that happen?" The immediate response was not an accurate interpretation of the reason why the facilitator won (we are talking about an extremely honest facilitator here); rather it was completely unsupported and false. So instead of moving on to the third question, the facilitator acknowledged the initial comment made but did not let the participants stop there. She continued on, asking the same question, just in a different way. By pressing the participants to really examine and understand why a particular behavior occurred, the facilitator enabled the group to learn relevant, accurate information as a result of the experience.

Consider another scenario in which the group is reluctant to own their behavior:

Facilitator: Did you notice that each person went down the same path and came to the same dead end? (Question 1)
Participant: Yes.
Facilitator: Why did that happen? (Question 2)
Participant: Because the path is confusing.
Facilitator: *Yes, and* what else might have caused everyone to make the same mistake? (Question 2 – restated)
Participant: Well, maybe they were scared that if they took a step in a different direction, the rest of the group would be mad at them.

In this example, the participant wanted to blame the hesitation on the path rather than the participants. Often participants look for a scapegoat in the activity itself rather than taking a risk and identifying themselves as culpable. The reality that every participant followed the same dead-end path is clear but does not really get to the heart of what else may have been going on with this activity. In this case, the facilitator simply acknowledged and then probed for additional explanations by asking another form of the question "Why did that happen?" The resulting conversation ought to lead to a more accurate and clear interpretation of the meaning behind the activity, such as how dangerous it is to blindly follow the masses or how important it is to think for yourself. As facilitators we want to encourage participation, help the discovery of accurate interpretation, and also help the group look more deeply at causation.

Restating Question 2 with the implication that you are asking "Why did this **really** happen?" will help uncover more learning for the group. It is important to understand that asking a group to probe deeper into the whys of an event can be powerful and therefore dangerous territory, especially if the group appears reluctant. Deciding to "push" a group or individual, inviting them to a deeper level, is a judgment call on the part of the facilitator. Rely on intuition and experience to discern if the group has gotten to the heart of a particular moment. A word of caution: Even the most experienced facilitators can be wrong. Allow yourself the confidence to press a group to really understand why a given behavior or feeling occurred, but also accept the humility of being wrong and moving on if the group is not seeing what you are seeing.

Once they are grounded in a working interpretation, then they are ready for Question 3.

Question 3: Does It Happen in Life?

With the first two questions we focus only on the specific experience, nothing else. It's the third question that invites the participant to generalize the experience, asking them to look at it in broader terms and see if there is any connection between the experience itself and what happens in their lives. If participants are only asked to think about and discuss the proximate experience, they have no opportunity to transfer any understanding or learning from the current experience into their own lives. The facilitator's job is to help the group uncover those connections by asking participants to consider how the activity could be relevant to them.

- Trying to help groups generalize their learning from a specific experience and acknowledge that there may be similarities in behavior elsewhere in their lives is something we have come to refer to as **"climbing over the wall of learning."** People who climb over the wall of learning are able to see the connection between an observation from an initial experience and a situation in the future. People who don't make it over the wall of learning are doomed to repeat the same lesson over and over again in a variety of different contexts.

While it is not difficult to learn a specific lesson, it is often a challenge for one to see how that single lesson matters in other areas of life. For instance, if you touch a hot pot on the stove and get burned, only a very minimal amount of brain connection is required not to touch the same pot on the same stove again. The real challenge comes in using the experience of touching the hot pot and the observation that it hurts to avoid touching other hot things regardless of shape, size, and material in the future.

Many times in a debriefing, a group will be able to easily identify what happened in the activity and may even be able to understand why it happened. However, it is not always easy for groups to make the connections between a simulated activity and events that happen in real life. It can be very difficult for a group to see that similar behaviors can happen in many different contexts and that the learning from one experience can possibly be generalized to many others. Many discussion models rely upon simple phrasing to create the generalization, like, "What do you learn from this?" Although direct and sometimes effective, we have seen many previously talkative groups go dead silent when this question is thrown out. Sometimes it is simply too broad or too intimidating to answer. Or perhaps it was asked at the wrong time in the debriefing process.

Another impediment to a successful group conversation happens when a facilitator jumps in to rescue a group that is struggling to find the answers and provides the "appropriate learning." Although this is an extremely tempting thing to do, we want to encourage you not to do it. Giving away "the answer" might make you feel better and more accomplished, and some group members might even grasp what you are saying. The facilitator's job, however, is not to process for the group but to invite group members to make the connections that will lead them to find their own powerful answers. Fight the temptation to "know" and instead work to become curious about what the group "knows." How will they answer the difficult questions about how their feelings and behaviors connect to other parts of their lives? By encouraging your group to struggle, you open up greater opportunities for long-lasting learning.

Within The 5 Questions approach, Question 3 is another closed-ended question that will help guide the participants to the next level. This is a specific and highly effective technique to help participants climb over the wall of learning and help them generalize their observations. As simple as it sounds, asking "Does it happen in life?" allows participants to easily connect the observation from the activity to similar observations made in other parts of their lives. Note the following debriefing:

> Facilitator: Did you notice how John was easily able to take leadership of the group? (Question 1)
> Participant: Yes. He did quickly become the leader.
> Facilitator: Why did that happen? (Question 2)
> Participant: He was the loudest and so we just started listening to what he said.
> Facilitator: Does that happen in life? Does the loudest person sometimes become the leader? (Question 3)
> Participant: Yes, that is often true. The loudest person can sway others toward their point of view, even when I know everyone disagrees.

Having anchored firmly in the experience as well as the specific observation from that experience, the facilitator is able to ask the group to reflect further. Ideally, Question 3 is phrased in such a way that participants can easily relate it to their own experience. If you are working with students, you might change the question to "Does that happen at school?" If you are working in a corporate setting, you may ask "Does that happen at work?" Bringing a specific context to mind will allow the participants to clearly connect the observation to their "real-life" experience and previous observations.

This phase of questioning opens up the **abstract conceptualization phase of learning**. At this point the task is to bring the participants out of the specific experience and into an observation of the patterns at work in themselves or other places. Without focused facilitation, participants may stay mired in their direct experience or may translate only the emotionally charged aspects of an experience, thus never being able to get over the wall of learning.

The following two scenarios could be the result of a highly emotionally charged experience where one member of the group is feeling hurt and slighted. Left to her own devices, it would be easy to imagine her reflecting in the following way:

> Facilitator: Did you notice you were frustrated during this experience? (Question 1)
> Participant: Yes, I hated it.
> Facilitator: Why did you hate it? (Question 2)
> Participant: Because these people are jerks. I wish I had never done this. I am not going to do this kind of experience again.
> Facilitator: How come? (Asking for explanation)
> Participant: Because it was so uncomfortable.
> Facilitator: What made you uncomfortable? (Question 2 again)
> Participant: Oh, I don't know. Maybe how rude people were or how they didn't want to help and ... I don't know; it was just terrible.

The participant correctly identified a powerful emotion, hate, then took only the briefest moment to reflect on the source of this emotion: "These people are jerks." That may be an accurate assessment based on her observation and judgment. Left to a facilitator who continues to focus on only the present moment, there really will be no opportunity for generalized learning to occur. Rather than having an opportunity to think about the way in which this experience could mirror her experience in other contexts, she simply shut down, having learned only one thing: that she will never again put herself into this kind of specific situation. In this scenario the participant is stuck on one side of the wall of learning, staying only in her interpretation of the experience and avoiding any connection to life beyond the experience. She will most likely not be able to get over the wall of learning without help. Without the right questions, this participant will not see patterns or connections between this situation and other situations in her real life. Therefore all opportunity for powerful, relevant, and meaningful learning is lost.

Now with another facilitator, the conversation might be entirely different.

> Facilitator: Did you notice that you were frustrated during this experience? (Question 1)
>
> Participant: Yes, I hated it.
>
> Facilitator: Why did you hate it? (Question 2)
>
> Participant: Because these people are jerks. I wish I had never done this. I am not going to do this kind of experience again.
>
> Facilitator: Does that happen to you sometimes at work? Do you have to work with people you don't like or do an assignment you don't like to do? (Question 3)
>
> Participant: Yeah, sometimes you have to work with people that you don't get along with and do things that aren't always what I would consider fun.

Rather than focusing exclusively on what a miserable time she is having in the immediate situation and what jerks these people are, she is now thinking about the fact that in other contexts similar observations can be made. She is climbing over the wall of learning and is now open to a variety of possible connections. She may choose to look at why she doesn't get along with people, or the specific triggers that set her bad feelings in motion. She may alternatively look more closely at how she might deal with people she doesn't like in more productive ways. Either way, the experience still holds out the opportunity for a generalized and hopefully useful connection.

Often groups and/or individuals have difficulty identifying and accepting aspects of their own behavior; this is where a facilitator can be especially helpful in guiding the group to recognize and discuss those blind spots. That is exactly the power of an experiential simulation or activity. A facilitator helps by asking the hard question, "Does that happen in life as well?" Although participants may struggle with the answer, this question can begin the group on a powerful journey.

Question 4: Why Does This Happen?

The function of this question is similar to that of Question 2. It exists to follow up on the commitment made in response to Question 3. Participants will acknowledge that they either do or do not see a connection between the specific experience and their everyday lives. Question 4 helps them tease out the patterns and causal relationships that underlie that connection.

> Facilitator: Did you notice how successful you were on the third try? (Question 1)
> Participant: Yes, that was awesome!
> Facilitator: Why did that happen? (Question 2)
> Participant: We stopped fighting about which was the "right" way and decided to just start trying ideas. That

really helped because we immediately started working together.
Facilitator: Does that happen in life? (Question 3)
Participant: Sure, sometimes.
Facilitator: Why does that happen? (Question 4)
Participant: Well, sometimes you need to stop talking about how to do stuff and just try it. By not wasting energy fighting, you have more energy to put into moving forward.

Notice how, in this example, the answer to Question 4 sounds very similar to the answer to Question 2. This is exactly as it should be and is one indication that the participant is climbing over the wall of learning.

The answer to "Why does that happen?" elaborates on the specific case and helps the group connect to the larger patterns at work. This can be a moment of profound learning. It should not be shortchanged or brushed past. Thoroughly understanding the "why" behind an observation will set up Question 5 and enable participants to be different when they approach the same topic again.

Question 5: How Can You Use That?

Finally, this is the heart of the issue. Fundamentally, the final question of any experiential exercise is "How will you be different in the future as a result of this experience?" It is important for participants to face this question head on and recognize the responsibility of using their newly acquired information. What is the difference between having information and not using it, and not having the information at all? The experience/question is useless unless it creates some impetus to modify behavior in the future. At this point in the process the participant often meets and must scale the second wall of learning.

The Wall of Learning (Take 2)

How many times have you made the same mistake twice? We are guessing more than once. Maybe it is a design flaw in our brains, or maybe this is exactly our task; either way, not applying what we have learned in the past to situations in the future appears to be endemic to human experience.

One reason why participants hit this second wall of learning is **fear**. Publicly stating their future intentions begins the process of making them accountable for change. Knowing it will require some changes on their part causes participants to anticipate the discomfort and anxiety that could be involved. As a facilitator, your objective is simply to provide a safe and supportive environment for them to make those declarations. State the question boldly and encourage participants to take it seriously.

Another reason that participants hit this second wall of learning is **ambiguity**. If they have not really understood the connection between their experience and the way in which they operate in the world, they cannot clearly state their intention to use that information. This requires the facilitator to back up and re-ask Questions 3 and 4. Encourage participants to really think about the connections and to draw conclusions that are meaningful to them in their experience.

For a learning to first transfer to long-term memory, and then be strong enough that it will change future behavior, requires that the brain's synaptic connections literally be changed. This can happen in a number of ways.

Repetition plays a major role in learning. Simply rehashing the same point in multiple ways and asking participants to continue to reflect on what they would do differently can create change. Sometimes we do not have the luxury of time and repetition, lest our participants get bored and we lose focus in the moment.

Emotion and intention are also significant contributors to learning. Getting participants to change their behavior in the future means associating the change as emotionally positive in some way – at a basic level, either pleasure-enhancing or pain-reducing. The opportunity for real change is further enhanced with stated intention. A shift occurs when a participant makes a bold statement such as, "Next time, I will check to make sure everyone has been heard." Making this statement reinforces the learning.

- **Where?** To help participants take a declaration to the next level we often ask the follow up question, **"Where specifically will that be useful?"** Giving a declaration context is a way of visualizing that future. We liken it to goal setting: The more specific you make the goal, the more clearly you "see" it, the more likely you are to achieve it.

Some participants may feel that it is redundant or intrusive to be pushed into making context-specific declarations. The following conversation can create some discomfort:

Facilitator: Why does that happen? (Question 4)
Participant: Because people are sometimes afraid to make a mistake. If you think people will judge you, then it is hard to decide when you know it might be wrong. I know it is not always the best thing, but that is what people do.

Facilitator: How can you use that? (Question 5)
Participant: Well, I try to just not care what people think. I make the best decision I can and try to move forward.
Facilitator: Where specifically will that be useful? (Question 5 – where?)
Participant: Uhhm. I guess I am thinking a lot about college right now. Everyone is giving me advice, but I don't think anybody really knows. I want to listen to everyone, but ultimately, it has to be my decision.

As the participant struggles to think about where the specific lesson would be useful, his/her mind begins to cycle through possibilities. It can often stop in places where eminent and difficult decisions need to be made, or powerful changes need to occur. Committing to a course of action in these places can be very difficult. We sometimes help participants through it by asking them if they think the lesson they learned or the connection they made was a good one. Recalling whether they like the direction of the debriefing to that point can solidify and reinforce the courage necessary to declare a future course of action.

Whether participants learn from experience in a way that they are changed can only be known by them. Our opportunity with "How can you use that?" is to help them fast-forward briefly and set down a path that might make change possible.

The 5 Questions — Working Together
The 5 Questions reveal a cycle, and in very rare circumstances, a group will actually follow the circular path. We have indeed had moments in a debriefing that are this simple:

Facilitator: Did you notice that I won every game?

Participant: Yes.

Facilitator: Why did that happen?

Participant: Because you have played it before. You know the strategy! If you know the strategy, it is easy to win.

Facilitator: Does that happen in life?

Participant: Of course!

Facilitator: Why does that happen?

Participant: Well, the person who knows the strategy has an advantage over the person who doesn't. That means they win more often.

Facilitator: How can you use that information?

Participant: Well, we try to use it every day. We are constantly working on our strategy. If we stay clear about our strategy, or if we can find a strategy that works more effectively than others, then we are likely to win.

This kind of conversation is rare. An innumerable amount of challenges arise in the course of a single debrief. People backtrack and repeat themselves. Different people are at different places in processing the information. They fail to make even obvious connections. They get stuck on particular ideas and themes.

The debriefing process challenges everyone. Like any skill, the more you practice it and pay attention to yourself, the better you get. If your practice involves giving away the answers, talking more than the group, or skipping questions, you will only make yourself better at unsuccessful methods.

With time, patience, and coaching, debriefing can become one of the more powerful tools in your educational tool kit.

It has the power to transform and enlighten. At its best, it takes the facilitator off the stage and puts each participant in touch with their own centers of knowledge and power.

Why 5? Why Not 4? Why Not 17?

We like the structure of five questions with the pattern of questioning following a closed, open, closed, open, open structure for a variety of reasons. The first is practical. As we attempted to teach both more and less complicated structures to new facilitators, they were often either not comprehensive enough or too comprehensive to be of practical value. The second is more theoretical. The five questions connect explicitly to each of the stages in the learning cycle in very conscious ways. We move deliberately and smoothly through observation, causation/interpretation, generalization, and application. This allows for a deliberate and open style of facilitation which has generated enormously productive conversations for us and the groups we have worked with.

Different trainers, researchers, and teachers have used different sets of questions to touch the same essential stops. Our objective here is to lay out one approach that we have found extremely useful across a wide variety of participants. Let us remind you that our approach is a road map and not a definitive, inflexible guide. The intention is to use The 5 Questions as a tool set that can guide a facilitative process. The more you use them and stay aware of the experience of debriefing, the more skilled you will become in knowing when to alter or embellish them.

| **Keep the Conversation Moving**

"BUT THIS BRIDGE WILL ONLY TAKE YOU HALFWAY THERE
– THE LAST FEW STEPS YOU'LL HAVE TO TAKE ALONE."
—Shel Silverstein

You know The 5 Questions, you have started asking them, and you have gotten some good answers. Then a silence falls over the group, or you notice that several people have tuned out. Sometimes participants want to contribute more or less information than is appropriate, or they want to communicate in a different way than the group requires. A variety of obstacles can prevent a group from moving forward.

A common denominator for many of these obstacles is the disconnection between what the group experience requires of participants and what participants want or are willing to contribute. When this happens, some level of tension is created. What do you do? The ability to effectively resolve that tension can be the difference between a good facilitator and a great one. This chapter is focused on sharing some of the techniques that have worked well for us.

Conflict and Resistance

Let's just put it out there. Conflict exists. People will dis-agree. They will get heated and emotional. It's okay. In fact, we know from studying group development that the most healthy and productive groups have conflicts and, through experience, figure out how to work through them. As a fa-cilitator, you must learn to embrace conflict and work with it. It won't help you or the group if your strategy is to avoid conflict. Go ahead; jump in.

Resistance, like conflict, will also emerge. For a variety of reasons, participants will be reluctant to participate. Your job as the facilitator is to determine how much to invite resistant group members into the conversation, and how much to let them be. It is trial and error and honing the skills of reading where people are in any given moment. That's the art of facili-tation. Following are some tools and strategies that will help you deal with both resistance and conflict in your groups.

"Tell Me More"

This is our all-time-favorite thing to say to encourage people to talk. Quiet or reluctant group members often need a bit of extra encouragement to elaborate on their thoughts and observations. Many participants contribute only the bare minimum unless invited to share more.

Curiously, it doesn't usually take much encouragement to get a person talking. Just the simple sentence "**Tell me more**" can do the trick. It is important that this request is made with absolute, genuine curiosity and authenticity. It's got to be real. If you don't actually want the person to tell you more and you stop listening midway through the telling, group members will take note and begin to

- shut down. Therefore, choose wisely when you ask to be told more.
- Make sure that you and the group are prepared to listen.

When conducting workshops with parents, the topic of the ritual after-school question will come up: "So, what did you do in school today?" The typical response is "Nothing" or a variation thereof. Our consistent advice to parents is to smile, lean forward, look their child in the eyes and say, "Wow, tell me more." Parents have reported that they found it amazing how much more their children had to say about "nothing."

We have discovered that many people are conditioned to believe that others don't really care about their opinion. Being marginalized and not really listened to is a daily experience for many of us. Naturally then in a group experience, people may not expect others to be interested in their comments. An honest "Tell me more" goes a long way toward convincing people that you are serious about wanting to hear what they have to say. The best encouragement participants can have is an appreciative, curious audience. It's fun to see people open up and relax into being heard.

- **Variations of "Tell me more":**
  - • Tell me more about that.
  - • What does that look like?
  - • Tell us more about that.
  - • Go on.
  - • Okay, and then what?

Silence
Silence is complex and inevitable. A skilled facilitator must be able to discern what the silence is about and respond appropri-

ately. It is important to become comfortable with the silence that is part of the rhythm of group processing. It is often in the quiet moments that creative solutions can emerge.

Silence can also be an indicator that the facilitator may have asked a question that was offtrack or unclear. You will need to trust your intuition and learn to read your group in order to determine what the situation is and how best to respond. We have provided you with some options to use when faced with silence. Figure 1 captures each of these possibilities.

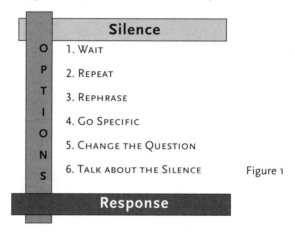

	Silence
O	1. WAIT
P	2. REPEAT
T	3. REPHRASE
I	4. GO SPECIFIC
O	5. CHANGE THE QUESTION
N	6. TALK ABOUT THE SILENCE
S	
	Response

Figure 1

Let there be silence.
Count to seven in your head to give them "think time." This will work when the silence exists because people are truly thinking. What an amazing feeling to be thinking so hard about a question that you are not aware of what others are doing. Thinking deeply about a question is an opportunity for deeper reflection. If you reach seven in your head, and no one as said anything, it is time to move to the next strategy.

Ask the question again.

If you are confident that your question has relevance for the group, then simply restate it. Saying it again can spark all kinds of new reflection in the group. On occasion we have noticed a silence that seemed so deep that the group was just reluctant to break it. When you restate the question, you break the silence and once again give the group permission to respond. If they don't respond quickly this time, it is time to move on. Do not wait for 7 seconds a second time. That is a sure way to turn a powerful, reflective silence into an awkward, oppressive silence.

Ask the question in a slightly different way.

You asked the group, "Why did that happen?" and got no response. Try rephrasing the question to make it more accessible: "So you noticed that no one took a leadership role; why do you think that no one stepped into that role?" By simply altering the way you asked the question, you could help the group think about it in a different way. If you are still getting nowhere, it is time for more dramatic action.

Go specific.

Ask a group member by name to answer the question. This is where the facilitator starts putting some skin in the game. By this point, the group has noticed the silence. Calling on a specific person will both remove the pressure from the group and place a lot more pressure on one single participant. Our experience suggests that you need to choose this person with some care. Look for the person who seems just on the verge of sharing but just needs a little push. When one person has spoken, it may help break the barrier for others. If the person you asked has a difficult time responding, then it is time to change your strategy. At some point we must acknowledge that the problem may not be in the group.

Change the question.
Assume it was a bad question. Go in a different direction. For example, imagine a teacher who shows a civil war video to her class. The video contains numerous themes as well as visual and statistical data. It may provoke all kinds of reactions within the class. When the lights come on, the teacher strides to the middle of the class and asks, "So, what did you learn from that?" She is amazed when the class is starkly silent. The problem here may not be that the class is not thinking; indeed they are likely processing a lot inside their minds. The problem is that she has asked a question about generalized learning while the class is still thinking about what it was they saw. They still need to publish and describe their experience. By changing the question to "Did you notice ..." or "What did you see in the video?" the teacher is more likely to receive a response.

Name the silence and talk about the silence.
"It's really quiet in here; what's going on?" Sometimes it turns out that the experience to be debriefed is the debriefing itself. We have had some of our most powerful moments as facilitators when we simply called the group out and named their behavior. Being a powerful observer should not end when the "experience" is over because truly the experience and the debriefing are not separate. What learning is available to the group when you name the silence?

What If You Did Know? Take a Guess.

The most common teenage response to virtually any question is "I don't know." We are constantly amazed by how little 15-year-olds seem to know. Funny, because most often, they do know. In reality, they are afraid of looking stupid, of not saying the right thing, or of being vulnerable in front of others. There is great feat in owning the knowledge they have, particularly in front of others.

"What if you did know?" is, more often than not, exactly the right thing to ask, and sure enough, with very little pause, you get a response. Here's an example:

> Facilitator: Why do you think most people sit in the same place every day at lunch?
> Participant: I don't know.
> Facilitator: What if you did know?
> Participant: Well, I don't know, I guess people maybe don't want to try new things. And, you know, once you get comfortable with one group, you don't really want to try anything else. I mean, what if the new group didn't like you?

The participant was reluctant to own the knowledge and opinion he had about people and their behavior. As the facilitator, the challenge is to listen very carefully to what the participant does own and know and then draw it out for exploration and learning.

This technique has to be used cautiously, especially with adult groups. The intention is not to "trick" the participant, but to bypass their internal critic that prevents them from "knowing." With certain people you will end up with the following exchange:

Facilitator: Why do you think most people sit in the same place every day at lunch?
Participant: I don't know.
Facilitator: What if you did know?
Participant: I just told you, I don't know!

When this happens, we have learned to smile and respond, "Great ... take a guess." It is amazing what good guessers most people are.

The bottom line for this kind of inquiry is to stay committed. "What if you did know?" and "Guess" are really just code language for "I really care about you and am honestly interested in what you have to say." By not allowing a participant to get away with "I don't know" when they truly do have some ability to answer, the facilitator moves conversation forward and builds trust in the group.

Gatekeep
Gatekeeping is being aware of the people who are quiet or shy and have not participated in the conversation. The facilitator can open the gate for the person to speak. At the right moment, you might direct a question to the quiet one. "Monica, what do you think about people supporting each other in the work place?" Don't get hung up on whether the person chooses to answer the question. What's important is making sure that everyone has the opportunity to share.

Boomerang
Often in the early stages of a group's debriefing it is common for group members to ask questions of and make comments to the facilitator rather than directly address one another. It

is the facilitator's job to help the group communicate with each other as directly as possible.

* **Boomeranging** is the art of giving a question or statement back to the group for their consideration and comments, rather than commenting on and answering all observations and questions yourself. The more challenging the question, observation, or statement, the more likely it will be directed toward the facilitator. This is because it can be easier to give away authority and knowledge than to risk owning it yourself. The challenge of the facilitator is to send the question, observation, or statement back to the group for pondering and exploration.

> Facilitator: Did you notice that, as a group, you all looked to Pete for leadership? (Question 1)
> Group: Yeah.
> Facilitator: Why did that happen? (Question 2)
> Participant: I'm not sure ... uh, is that common for groups to do?
> Facilitator: That's a good question; what do you all think about that?

Another scenario for boomeranging in the context of The 5 Questions could also look like this:

> Facilitator: Did you notice that, as a group, you all looked to Pete for leadership? (Question 1)
> Group: Yeah.
> Facilitator: Why did that happen? (Question 2)
> Participant 1: I think it's because we are not that good at working together and so Pete just took over.
> Facilitator: Is that true at work? (Question 3)

Group: Yeah.

Facilitator: Why does this happen?

Participant 2: Because when a group can't figure out what to do to be a better team, I think that it starts looking for help or someone to be in charge so that we can at least get our work done.

Facilitator: What do you all think about that? Is it true that we naturally want someone else to be in charge when we can't figure it out on our own?

Instead of going straight to Question 5, the facilitator put Participant 2's comment out to the group and asked for input on the observation without asserting his own opinion. It is important for you as the facilitator to pay attention. Are you answering/responding to more questions than the group? If so, use the boomerang technique and send those questions back to the group.

Reframing

When a group gets particularly stuck or conflict feels too hard, use your perspective as an outsider to reframe the issue. For example, imagine a group stuck on whether it would have been better to cooperate or compete to achieve the best result. As you listen to the exchange of ideas, you may see a middle way that enables the group to get unstuck. You might reframe the issue away from either/or to both/and. For example, "Instead of competing or cooperating, could aspects of both have relevance?"

When participants get fixated on small issues, it is helpful for the facilitator to zoom out on the issue and reframe the problem in the context of what is best for the big picture.

Alternatively, sometimes you need to reframe by zooming in. For example, a group is going in circles about what effective leadership should look like. The facilitator can reframe by asking the group to think about a particular work context. Framing the conversation through the viewpoint of a project manager, verses the viewpoint of the division president, can have a dramatic impact on the way the group understands the debriefing. As a facilitator, your task is to ensure that you frame the issues in a way that works for the group and promotes understanding on all sides.

What If

Another of our favorite techniques is to ask, "What if?" It has so many varied and interesting applications that we challenge you to look for appropriate places to insert it.

- **"What if?" is just a plain, powerful question.** It helps participants explore different angles of the topic at hand. "What if" questions invite the group to notice what didn't happen in a particular scenario and, as a result, ponder alternative possibilities.
  - What if you all cooperated?
  - What if you had asked for outside support?
  - What if you attempted this entirely by yourself?

Dichotomies

Is that good or bad? Did that help or hurt? Are you moving forward or backward? Contrasts force people to choose and then explore why they chose what they did. Differing opinions open the opportunity for participants to take a stand on an issue and then explore their rationale.

We like introducing an either/or choice in the generalization aspect (Question 4 of the learning cycle). This is when participants are grappling with the significance of the learning in which they are engaged. Notice the following exchange:

Facilitator: Did you notice that I never assigned teams? (Question 1)

Participant: That's right, you never did; we just formed teams on our own!

Facilitator: Why did that happen? (Question 2)

Participant: Well, it seemed like there were limited resources, so we just organized ourselves in a way that would allow us to win the simulation.

Facilitator: Does that happen in life? (Question 3)

Participant: Absolutely. We often align ourselves to compete when we perceive that there are limited resources.

Facilitator: Is that good or bad? (Dichotomy)

Having generalized the experience, we can ask participants to delve into the notion of whether they are engaging in behaviors in which they want to continue. This can lead to fascinating and powerful conversations. At the same time, we realize that this kind of forced dichotomy is not always appropriate. Few choices are truly either/or, and the world is full of shades of gray.

Accept/Legitimize/Deal With/Defer

Negative comments and distractions are the most difficult things to handle as a facilitator. In approaching these potential roadblocks, we recognize four available choices. First, you can **accept** it. Sometimes by accepting the world as it presents itself, warts and all, you can move past it. Accepting a negative comment is essentially to do nothing. You give minimal response, simply accept that the comment was made, and move on.

To **legitimize** is to give a positive response to a negative situation. Call it out and acknowledge the reality of the situation. For example, a student says, "This is stupid." You agree wholeheartedly with, "Yes, this is really stupid." This counter-intuitive response can often take a negative person by surprise. By legitimizing their complaint, you may be able to open them to seeing that although they are right, they may not be paying attention to the whole picture.

To **deal with** a negative comment requires additional tools and time. When you decide to take on a negative comment or situation, you are setting yourself up to battle, and in some cases there can only be one winner. Proceed with extreme caution when directly confronting a negative person.

To **defer** negativity can often be the most effective strategy, especially when you are pressed for time. Our advice is to trust the process of debriefing. Often participants who start out negative or resistant eventually come to see enormous value in the conversation. Some even become active participants. When you defer, you need to trust that the negativity will not infect the rest of the group and that the process will work to shift the negative participants.

Humor
Laughter is a powerful, unifying force in any group. Humor can cut through tension and shift the energy dramatically. We encourage you to use it! If you aren't a naturally "funny

person," then become adept at noticing the inborn humor and fabulous absurdity of life that can be found in almost any group or situation at some point.

It is important to avoid humor that is sarcastic or at someone's expense, especially as a facilitator. Damage to group trust happens quickly and is difficult to repair once the damage is done.

Get Up and Move

At times the conversation has gone on so long and been so intense that participants just need to get up and move around in order to refocus and reenergize. Give them permission to get up and stretch.

Play a quick game, do crazy kinetics – such as jumping jacks or a hand jive, switching chairs or places in the circle, or just running around the room. Get the blood flowing and the ideas will again flow freely.

Take a Break

Sometimes just moving around isn't enough to get the group refocused. Take a break and come back to the topic after people have a chance to get some food, go to the bathroom, walk around a bit, etc. It's important that you pay attention and take care of the group in this way. On the other hand, use breaks judiciously. Once the group breaks, it can be difficult to pull them back. Before letting them go, give a restart time and be prepared to walk around and pull them back to the circle when it's time to start again.

Dialogue

One last thing we want to mention before we end this chapter is dialogue. Dialogue is a process for conversation described aptly by physicist David Bohm, among others. Bohm defines dialogue as a process to use in groups to help people understand one another and their thoughts. The process often leads to uncovering deeply held assumptions about culture, meaning, and identity.

It is our hope that after reading this book and using The 5 Questions, you will be curious to learn more about facilitation and deeply transformative conversation. The process of good dialogue can teach us much about how to listen to one another and engage in powerful conversation with one another. A few of the key concepts used in dialogue are listed here to provoke interest.

Suspend your own beliefs and assumptions.

Invite participants to really explore why the person speaking arrived at their belief. Encourage them to more deeply hear and potentially understand one another. This is a challenging objective, and when you are successful, the level of discovery and exploration that results is awesome.

Balance inquiry with advocacy.

Advocacy is when you put energy toward explaining your own point of view or experience. Inquiry is when you suspend your own views and actively seek to understand someone else's point of view. In dialogue, it is important for all participants to be aware of the roles of advocacy and inquiry, the intention being to balance between the two and learn what each mode feels and looks like. In this way we can actually have dialogue, instead of two monologues taking place back and forth.

Different points of views are welcomed and explored.

By discovering/discerning our differences, we can learn more about one another. This is still an uncommon approach to divergent thinking, and it is exciting when groups learn to welcome thinking that is not similar. Amazing new pathways to creativity and learning can open up.

Dialogue can be playful and fun!

That's part of our attraction to dialogue as a process. It's deep and transformational, and it's fun to be a part of! There are dialogue groups all over the country, and many books about the process are available. We hope you are curious to discover more about dialogue. Please refer to the bibliography for further information.

Chapter Five | **Make It Experiential!**

"IT'S NOT THE SAME TO TALK OF BULLS, AS TO BE IN THE
BULLRING." —Spanish Proverb

How many times have we watched an earnest presenter stand and lecture about how important it is for participants to *experience* their learning? We believe that it is imperative to teach debriefing and closure through experience. Better to memorize and practice The 5 Questions in the safe confines of a workshop than during a live debriefing.

We have taught The 5 Questions to thousands of new facilitators – young and old, experienced and inexperienced. In fact, every fall, over 60,000 high school and middle school facilitators use The 5 Questions method to help create meaning around activities for freshmen and 6th graders during their transition to a new school. The activities and workshops here were developed in support of the Link Crew and WEB programs. We are deeply indebted to those programs for giving us reason to create The 5 Questions and allowing us the space and time to develop and refine them over the last 10 years.

This workshop was designed for beginning facilitators, although we have used it with more advanced facilitators as well. Camp counselors, outdoor experience facilitators, teachers, counselors, and staff development professionals will find this workshop most beneficial. When a group already has a functional understanding of the learning cycle and/or other questioning methodologies like Bloom's Taxonomy or Socratic Dialog, then the conversation about how The 5 Questions might be useful can be extremely rich.

The 5 Questions workshop is designed to be conducted in a 60-minute block. Like you, we are often time-constrained in our work and always seek to make the most impact in the least amount of time. A certain degree of pacing and timing are required to combine engaged fun in the moment with long-term, lasting impact. We have borrowed the activities that we use in these workshops from a wide variety of sources. Please keep in mind that this book is not intended to be an experiential activities and games book.

If you are working with new facilitators that will shortly be responsible for using this material, it is helpful to build in some level of assessment. We have found **assessing a facilitator's skill** to be one of the most challenging aspects of teaching this methodology. Many people tend to overestimate their skill in facilitation. As we have few models of how it ought to look, and each experience is distinct from the previous one, it can be difficult to determine mastery. Nonetheless, finding a way to observe and provide immediate feedback to new facilitators is critical. We highly encourage a program of observation to ensure that what you are teaching is actually being learned and applied. Brain research reveals that the

- old adage is indeed true: Practice does not make perfect; perfect
- practice makes perfect. The longer a new facilitator goes without
- feedback to improve, the more likely s/he is to get stuck in non-
- productive patterns.

The 5 Questions Workshop Outline

Introduction

Activity: Slap Hands

- Setup
- Play
- Guided debrief

Lecture: The Power of Setting Up Learning

Lecture: The 5 Questions

- First step – memorize

Activity: Orchestra

- Memorizing activity

Activity: Quiz

- Memorizing activity

Activity: Fast Fingers

- Choose teams of 3, designate A, B, & C
- A debriefs, B & C play

Lecture: Noticing

Activity: Push Pull

- B debriefs, A & C play

Lecture: Genuine Curiosity

Activity: Gotcha
> • C debriefs, A & B play

Activity: Count Off
> • Groups of 8 practice, designate 1 to debrief

The 5 Questions Workshop

Purpose: to teach The 5 Questions debriefing methodology and allow participants an opportunity to practice

Time Required: 60 minutes

Materials Required: None

Introduction •

Main Points:
- Introduce the workshop.
- Prepare for experiences.

Say This: "Welcome to the fun of debriefing experiential activities. Our objective in the next hour is to provide you with the basic framework for asking great questions as well as the opportunity to practice your skill.

"We cannot do a workshop about experience without having a few experiences, so with that brief introduction, let's get started."

Activity: Slap Hands • • • • • • • • • • • • • • • •

Procedure: "Please stand up and choose a partner." (Use any method of pairing people that you wish – keep time constraints in mind.) "Once you have a partner, please stand facing each other. One partner place both hands palms up about waist high. The other person now place your hands, palms down, over your partner's. You should now be palm to palm.

"Ready. Go." (Carefully observe the reaction of the group when you say "go." Do not give any further instructions. After a few minutes, get the group's attention again.)

"Go ahead and sit down. Please turn to your partner and talk about that experience for a moment. What did you notice as you were playing?" (Let the pairs discuss for a few minutes.)

QUESTIONS:
- Did you notice that I did not actually tell you which game to play? (Question 1)
- Why did most of you play the same game? (Question 2)
- Does that happen in life? (Question 3)
- Why does that happen? (Question 4)
- How could we use that as facilitators? (Question 5)

Note: This is a guided debrief. As we are in more of a training mentality, we are not as open to outcome as we might be during a more open experience. Here it is helpful for participants to notice that experience guides action, and that by setting the group up in a particular way, you get a predictable response.

Lecture: The Power of Setting Up Learning
MAIN POINTS:
- Setup can predict outcome.
- Use setup in debriefing to ask the right questions at the right times.

SAY THIS: "The set up was critical for this activity, right? Part of our success as facilitators is our ability to set up experiences that will enable people to reflect on their actions and feelings. Notice that how you set up learning can often predict the kind of learning experience you will have. The setup is critical.

"As facilitators, our job is to set up our groups to be reflective and engaged about their own learning. We are not necessarily going to tell them what to learn, just as in this last activity, I didn't tell you what to play. Rather, we are going to create an environment for learning, ask questions that make it possible, and then guide our groups toward powerful connections."

Lecture: The 5 Questions ● ● ● ● ● ● ● ● ● ● ●

MAIN POINTS:
- You must first memorize these questions in order to be able to use them effectively later.
    1) Did you notice ... ?
    2) Why did that happen?
    3) Does that happen in life?
    4) Why does that happen?
    5) How can you use that?

SAY THIS: "To help set up learning, we need to learn five critical questions. These questions are mapped against how the brain processes and learns from experience. When asked with the right degree of skill, they unlock the learning potential in each of the experiences we will do with our groups. The 5 Questions are:
    1) Did you notice ... ?

2) Why did that happen?
3) Does that happen in life?
4) Why does that happen?
5) How can you use that?

"Each of these questions works together to help groups connect their experiences with each other to the experience of their lives. These connections create the environment for learning.

"Consider a little boy who burns his hand by touching a hot pot on a stove. He first notices the pain in his hand. He immediately starts to wonder why and thinks about the pot. Correctly making the connection between the hot pot and the pain in his hand allows him to consider that all hot things, especially when they are on a stove, might cause pain. This generalization will now guide his future experience with hot things. Hopefully he will no longer touch them. By consciously visiting each of these points on the 'learning cycle,' we help our groups create their own meaning from experience.

"Now let's turn our attention to actually memorizing these questions."

Activity: Orchestra ● ● ● ● ● ● ● ● ● ● ● ● ● ● ●

PROCEDURE: "Music is a powerful tool for memorizing. Notice how you can hear a song on the radio and have it stick in your head for hours afterward? We are going to use the power of song to help us remember The 5 Questions. Each question will have its own tune.

"First up is, 'Did you notice ... ?'" (Use an operatic style, or make up a tune that works for you.)

"Let's practice. When I point to you, sing out loud!" (They sing.) "Great first attempt; now let's do it with real gusto! Again!" (They sing louder.)

"Okay great, now the second question, 'Why did that happen?'" (Use a jazzy, low key, finger-snapping version.)

"Now the third question, 'Does it happen in life?'" (Use a rap/hip hop motif.)

"Now the fourth question, 'Why does that happen?'" (Repeat the jazzy refrain from Question 2)

"Finally, the fifth question, our capstone, 'How can you use that?'" (Use a pounding rocker melody complete with air guitar. [We are indebted to our colleague Mary Beth Campbell for enlightening us to the simplicity and utter ferocity of the rocker/air guitar riff.])

"Now that everyone knows the tunes, I am going to divide the group into five sections. Each section will take a different question, and I will conduct our 5 Questions masterpiece!" (Give all five groups a chance to practice their piece, then you conduct the orchestra. Have the groups go one at a time so that everyone gets to hear and appreciate each question.)

"Give yourselves a round of applause. Phenomenal music was just made! Mentally review each of The 5 Questions to see if they have begun to sink in."

Activity: Quiz • • • • • • • • • • • • • • • • • • •

Procedure: "The real test as to whether you have learned The 5 Questions will be if you can accurately remember them tomorrow. However, just to see if you are on the way, here comes a pop quiz!

"Please stand and give us question #1." (Point to one participant at random.)

"Group, let's give them a thunderous applause!! I mean really ridiculously over-the-top applause!!"

Ask people at random to stand and recite one of the questions. Gently correct them if they are wrong – in our experience they are rarely incorrect at this point, especially with other group members whispering the answer if they seem to be struggling. Continue to provide overwhelming applause to reinforce the fun and safety of this impromptu quiz.

Finally, ask one or two people to recite the entire five questions in order. Give these people a standing ovation.

Activity: Fast Fingers • • • • • • • • • • • • • • • •

Procedure: "Now that you know The 5 Questions in order, we need to give you an opportunity to practice with them. Please get into a group of three, and designate a person 'A,' a person 'B,' and a person 'C.'

"Person A, for this first activity you will be the observer and then you will debrief the activity using The 5 Questions. That means that you need to pay attention to the activity as your partners are playing. Notice their interaction, their feelings, and their behaviors. Any one of these things might be a good source for you to use with 'Did you notice ...?'

"B and C, you will play Fast Fingers. First, put both hands behind your back. On the count of three, each of you will bring your hands in front of you, displaying a certain number of fingers. The number that you choose to display is up to you. You might choose to hold out three fingers or nine fingers. With each of you showing your fingers, your challenge is to add up the total on both your hands and your partner's hands and then be the first to yell out that total. If your partner shows four fingers and you show three, then the person to yell 'seven' first is the winner. Any questions? Great, let's play! 1, 2, 3, go!" (Play three or four rounds.)

"Person A now debriefs the activity. Remember to start with a powerful observation following 'Did you notice...?'" (Person A debriefs for 5 minutes.)

QUESTIONS:
- Would a couple of groups raise their hands and let us know the different ways you started the debriefing?
- What were some of the first "Did you notice ...?" questions?

Lecture: Noticing
(For more on observation, see Chapter 3)
  MAIN POINTS:
  - What you notice dramatically impacts the quality of your debriefing.

• Some things are better to notice than others.

SAY THIS: "Did you notice that the way you phrase the first question sets the tone and direction for the debriefing? That ought to indicate to us that what we notice is critical. Notice what you are noticing right now. Many of you are focused on me, but some might still be thinking about the activity or the debriefing. Others are noticing different aspects of the room or maybe a nagging headache or other body pain. You may even notice that as I ran through that list, your attention shifted through the different things I was calling out, finally resting in that nagging pain in your body! Our attention is critical. Every moment of our life we are processing a huge amount of stimulation. Most of it is unremarkable and gets little attention."

When you watch a group in a structured experience, where does your attention go? What kinds of things do you notice? Here are a couple of reliable places to start each time you are facilitating a group.

Leadership: Who took leadership? Did the group accept them? Why? Were they effective?

Conflict: How did the group get along? What kinds of conflict were present? Was there a conflict between what the group wanted to achieve and what they actually achieved?

Communication: How well did the group communicate? Was everyone's opinion respected? Who tended to make the decisions? Was anyone left out? Why?

Activity: Push Pull ● ● ● ● ● ● ● ● ● ● ● ● ● ● ●

PROCEDURE: "For this next activity, B will observe and debrief while A and C play. This activity is called Push Pull. A and C need to stand on one foot. While you are standing on one foot, grab hands in a fireman's grip, with each holding the other's wrist. The objective is to strategically try to push or pull your opponent off balance. Ready, go!"

After A and C have played, B debriefs.

Lecture: Genuine Curiosity ● ● ● ● ● ● ● ● ● ● ● ● ●

MAIN POINT:

• Cultivating a spirit of curiosity brings more meaning to your debriefing.

SAY THIS: "What were you curious about as you were asking questions? Did you already believe you knew the answers? When you facilitate an activity, see what happens if you adopt a position of genuine curiosity. This means that you ask questions that you are genuinely curious about. Connect with the spirit of your internal five-year-old. That little kid inside of you that expresses endless curiosity. As you debrief and ask questions, notice if you are really curious or just walking through the motions. Think through The 5 Questions in your mind. Connect with the spirit of your five-year-old to ask questions in such a way that you become truly curious at every turn."

Activity: Gotcha • • • • • • • • • • • • • • • • • • •

PROCEDURE: "For our final triad activity, A and B will play while C gets a chance to debrief. A and B face each other and take your right hand and place it palm up toward your partner. Now take your left index finger and point it down directly in the center of your partner's palm. On the count of three, you will try to grab your partner's index finger and at the same time try to keep your index finger from being captured. 1, 2, 3, go!"

Person C now debriefs that experience.

Activity: Count Off • • • • • • • • • • • • • • • •

PROCEDURE: "Now that each of you has had an opportunity to debrief an experience, the challenge is to facilitate a group through an experience.

"I need each of the teams of three to join with two other groups to make groups of nine people each. In each group, designate a facilitator who will observe and debrief the entire group through this last experience.

"For the group, your challenge is to count from one to twenty. Simple enough. There are, however, some rules:

1. Everyone must say at least one number.
2. The group may not go in an organized pattern, for instance just going around the circle. The numbers must be random.
3. No one may indicate to any person when they should or should not say a number. No subtle coughs or pointing to help out. Each person must decide for themselves when they will say a number.

4. No two people can say the same number at the same time. If this happens, the entire group must start over from one.

"Ready. Begin." (Groups play for 5 - 7 minutes.)

"Facilitators, it is now your opportunity to provide closure for your group on that experience. Start with 'Did you notice ...?' and move smoothly through The 5 Questions. Go!"

References

BOOKS

Bloom, B., Englehart, M., Furst, E., Hill, W. & Krathwohl, D. (1956). *Taxonomy of educational objectives: The classification of educational goals*. Handbook I: Cognitive domain. New York, Toronto: Longmans, Green.

Bohm, D. (1996). *On dialogue*. New York, NY: Routledge.

Brookfield, S. D. (1986). *Understanding and facilitating adult learning*. San Francisco, CA: Jossey-Bass.

Cozolino, L. (2002). *The neuroscience of psychotherapy*. New York, NY: Norton and Company.

Dewey, J. (1938). *Experience and education*. New York, NY: Touchstone.

Dilts, R. (2003). *From coach to awakener*. Cupertino, CA: Meta Publications.

Garmston, R. & Wellman, B. (1997). *The adaptive school, developing and facilitating collaborative groups*. El Dorado Hill, CA: Four Hats Press.

Isaacs, W. (1999), *Dialogue and the art of thinking together*. New York, NY: Doubleday.

Kaner, S. (1996). *Facilitator's guide to participatory decision-making*. Gabriola Island, BC, Canada: New Society Publishers.

Kolb, D. A. (1984). *Experiential learning*. Englewood Cliffs, NJ: Prentice Hall.

Kotulak, R. (1996). *Inside the brain*. Kansas City, MO: Andrew McMeel Publishing.

Levine, M. (2002). *A mind at a time*. New York, NY: Simon & Schuster.

Luria, A. R. (1973). *The working brain*. New York, NY: Basic Books.

Neisser, B. & Saran, R. (2004). *Enquiring minds: Socratic dialogue in education*. Stoke on Trent, ST4 5NP, United Kingdom, Trentham Books Limited.

Thompson, J. (2004). *CASC staff development leadership handbook*. CASC.

WEB SITES

Experiential Learning Cycles, James Neill. www.wilderdom.com/ experientiallearningcycle.htm, Sept. 5, 2003.

Experiential Learning Articles and Critiques of David Kolb's Theory, Tim Pickles. http://reviewing.co.uk/research/experiential. learning.htm, April 14, 2004.

The Experiential Learning Cycle. www.dmu.ac.uk/~jamesa/ learning/experien.htm. April 14, 2004

Contextual/Natural Learning. www.humanoptions.com/learning. html, March 4, 2004.

What is Experiential Learning? www.teamskillstraining.co.uk/ tst_article1.htm, March 24, 2004.

Learning Theories and Transfer of Learning. www.otec.uoregon. edu/learning_theory.htm, Nov. 24, 2003

Learning from Experience. www.learningfromexperience.com Hit the Research Library, this takes you to several Kolb articles and the link to a 160-page bibliography on experiential learning theory.

About the Authors

Micah Jacobson has presented to over 800,000 students, educators, and parents throughout North America since 1990. He has been a trainer for the United Nation Youth Forum, The Association of Young Leaders in Russia, and for Columbine High School in Colorado. The core of Micah's work has always been experiential education.

As a cofounder of The Boomerang Project, Micah manages its nationally recognized transition and orientation programs, Link Crew and WEB. Link Crew and WEB together reach more than half a million freshmen and 6th graders each fall in more than 1,200 schools nationwide, helping to create positive school climates where kids feel comfortable, engaged, and successful. The Boomerang Project also produces outstanding faculty in-service, teacher training, and Open to Outcome Workshops.

Micah holds an MBA from the University of Michigan and in addition to working in education has been a manager for both consulting and technology companies. His passion continues to be working to help people engage more actively in their own lives.

Mari Ruddy is a School Development Consultant for The Big Picture Company, a nonprofit organization that supports small, innovative experiential high schools in primarily urban communities throughout the country. Big Picture Schools emphasize real world learning, personalized curriculum, and learning through one's interests and passions. Mari coaches principals and advisers in adapting to this innovative way of doing school.

Before Big Picture, Mari was a high school Spanish teacher for six years. She also ran a highly experiential leadership and student council program for six years. Mari was a high school administrator at a comprehensive high school for four years, during which time she oversaw proactive discipline programs that engaged students in the running of the school. For two years, Mari worked at the University of California, Santa Cruz in the Educational Partnership Center facilitating teams of teachers and professors in a pipeline of schools, helping them figure out how to level the playing field and raise the bar for kids who would not usually go to college.

Mari is also a popular youth development speaker and trainer, specializing in school culture and climate. She has worked in team building and leadership training with a wide variety of organizations from education to the corporate world. Mari has been teaching The 5 Questions model to adult and student facilitators for the past 12 years. She earned an MA in Educational Leadership from San Jose State University. Mari currently lives and plays in Denver, Colorado.

Open to Outcome
Workshops/Programs

Open to Outcome workshops are powerful learning experiences that give teachers, facilitators, camp directors and outdoor educators all the tools they need to lead and debrief experiential activities. Getting people actively engaged in learning opens the door to incredible, life changing moments. Facilitators are trained to gently guide participants toward internal reflection by using an open ended questioning model that helps them discover the learning that is true for them.

In the *Open to Outcome* workshop, we go beyond the text to engage facilitators and educators in a step by step guide to not only debriefing an experience, but also presenting and developing powerful material.

In the course of two days you will master:
- Designing Experiential Curriculum and Workshops
- Setting Up Powerful Learning Experiences
- More than 15 Hands-on Activities
- The 5 Questions Model of Debriefing
- Learning Cycle and Group Development Theory

Open to Outcome is also available as a powerful faculty in-service program. Programs can be designed to fit partial or whole day agendas.

For more information about booking an *Open to Outcome* workshop, please contact:

> The Boomerang Project
> PO Box 600
> Santa Cruz, CA 95061
> 831-460-7040 • 800-688-7578
> www.boomerangproject.com
>
> Micah Jacobson
> micah@boomerangproject.com
>
> Mari Ruddy
> mari@mariruddy.com